REAL-TIME DIPLOMACY

REAL-TIME DIPLOMACY

Politics and Power in the Social Media Era

Philip Seib

REAL-TIME DIPLOMACY
Copyright © Philip Seib, 2012.

All rights reserved.

First published in 2012 by
PALGRAVE MACMILLAN®
in the United States—a division of St. Martin's Press LLC,
175 Fifth Avenue, New York, NY 10010.

Where this book is distributed in the UK, Europe and the rest of the world,
this is by Palgrave Macmillan, a division of Macmillan Publishers Limited,
registered in England, company number 785998, of Houndmills,
Basingstoke, Hampshire RG21 6XS.

Palgrave Macmillan is the global academic imprint of the above companies
and has companies and representatives throughout the world.

Palgrave® and Macmillan® are registered trademarks in the United States,
the United Kingdom, Europe and other countries.

ISBN: 978–0–230–33942–2 (hc)
ISBN: 978–0–230–33943–9 (pbk)

Library of Congress Cataloging-in-Publication Data

Seib, Philip M., 1949–
    Real-time diplomacy : politics and power in the social media era / Philip Seib.
        p. cm.
    ISBN 978–0–230–33942–2 (hardcover : alk. paper)—
    ISBN 978–0–230–33943–9 (pbk. : alk. paper)
    1. Diplomacy—Technological innovations. 2. Diplomacy—Decision making—
Technological innovations. 3. Social media—Political aspects. 4. Internet and
international relations. 5. Protest movements in mass media. 6. Protest
movements—Arab countries—History—21st century. I. Title.

JZ1405.S45 2012
327.2—dc23   2011041553

A catalogue record of the book is available from the British Library.

Design by Newgen Imaging Systems (P) Ltd., Chennai, India.

First edition: April 2012

10 9 8 7 6 5 4 3 2 1

Printed in the United States of America.

To all those who went into the streets in the cause of freedom during the Arab Awakening of 2011.

When people choose to live,
Fate will have to respond,
Night will fade into day,
And shackles will be broken.

Abu Al Qasim Al Shabi (Tunisian poet, 1909–1934)

There is something in the soul that cries out for freedom.

Martin Luther King, Jr.

CONTENTS

ACKNOWLEDGMENTS

With the Arab Awakening very much underway as this book was written, keeping track of changing events was never easy. I owe great thanks to my research assistant, Arezou Rezvani, for her tireless work.

Along with Arezou, Sherine Badawi Walton read the manuscript as it developed and provided many useful insights. Amelia Arsenault offered her great knowledge of networks to help me shape the material on that topic. Maria Dayton's inside perspective on Arab reform movements was most helpful. Ziza Kamal introduced me to the writings of Abu Al Qasim Al Shabi, a passage from whose work is part of this book's epigraph, and Ezzeddine Abdelmoula helped me with the translation of it.

At the University of Southern California (USC), I have always received wonderful support from the leadership of the Annenberg School for Communication and Journalism—Ernie Wilson, Geneva Overholser, and Larry Gross—which makes working here a pleasure. In USC's School of International Relations, Laurie Brand's insights about Arab politics were helpful as I shaped the book. Most of all, I want to thank my colleagues at USC's Center on Public Diplomacy, who are always a delight to work with and who never flinched when I declared, "It's writing time!" and disappeared for days at an end.

At Palgrave Macmillan, Farideh Koohi-Kamali and Sarah Nathan are a wonderful team, and I appreciate their quick and thorough endorsement of the idea behind this book.

Most of all, I would like to thank the people whose courage was on display in the streets of the Arab world and whose embrace of freedom inspired this book. I know only a few of them, but I feel that I know them all. They have changed the world, with ramifications we cannot yet appreciate, and I am indebted to them.

INTRODUCTION

The Arab Awakening of 2011 was wonderful to behold. The established order, unresponsive and often cruel, suddenly found its control of public life slipping away. Energized by unprecedented connectivity to information sources and like-minded fellow citizens, those who had remained silent for so long in Tunisia, Egypt, and elsewhere found their voices and raised a din that caused the walls of autocracy to crack and then crumble in some places. In other Arab countries, the powerful, using force or cunning (or a mixture of the two), retained control, at least for the time being.

Regardless of short-term outcomes, the significance of these uprisings extends far beyond the Arab states where they occurred. As always, the dynamics of the Middle East affect the rest of the global community, and in this instance we will see lasting change in the ways that international relations are conducted.

Among the lessons deserving attention are the following:

- Democracy remains appealing, and people are still willing to put their lives on the line to attain it.
- As the venues of mass communication become more diverse and pervasive, individual citizens become intellectually and politically empowered. They know more about what is going on around them and they use media tools to form communities of interest that enhance political activism.
- Governments must learn to cope with political developments that proceed at an ever faster pace. Even the "24-hour news cycle" has become archaic because it relied on a finite number of information providers whose content could be monitored by policymakers with relative ease. Now the information sources are so dispersed and numerous that governments trying to keep up with events lack systematic ways to digest and judge information, and their policymaking becomes hesitant and reactive.

This book is not a chronicle of the Arab Spring and its immediate aftermath, but rather is an analysis of what the uprisings and the changes they reflect mean in the context of diplomatic practice. That is not to say that the dynamism of Tahrir Square was a transient phenomenon with little lasting effect on how governments do business. Rather, as the people of the revolutionary Arab states build new institutions designed to improve their nations and their lives, governments elsewhere cannot afford to assume that the spirit behind dramatic social change will now recede into history and that business as usual will resume. The political energy evident in the Arab world in 2011 and its effectiveness in bringing about reform might be replicated elsewhere, and policymakers within and outside the states where this takes place must be better prepared to respond.

Policymakers cannot be mere spectators. Stunned surprise is an inadequate response to transformative events, and yet that is what we saw from the United States and other major powers as events in the Arab world unfolded. President Barack Obama and other world leaders tried to act as change was occurring, but they always seemed to be behind the curve. Part of the problem was flawed intelligence analysis that overestimated the staying power of Egyptian president Hosni Mubarak and others, and reaction was also slowed by the recognition that the long-established alliances with autocratic regimes were suddenly proving untenable. But the main difficulty was the inability of the foreign policy decision-making process to keep pace with developments taking place on Arab streets and to understand the new information ecology within which change was fostered.

A fundamental incompatibility exists between speed and diplomacy. Effective diplomacy cannot be done on the fly; it requires back-and-forth among parties, an ability to listen and respond carefully. During much of the twentieth century, speed steadily encroached on diplomatic process as radio, then television, and then the Internet were increasingly relied upon by the public and policymakers as principal sources of information. The diplomatic pouch became largely obsolete as foreign ministries turned first to open sources such as the BBC, CNN, and, more recently, Twitter and its siblings to find out what was going on in distant parts of the world.

But even reports from the most highly regarded news organizations are not always correct, particularly when journalistic standards are compromised in the pursuit of getting a story first rather than first getting it right. Governments have their own information-gathering mechanisms, in the form of diplomats and intelligence agencies, but when much of the world seems to be moving at the same breakneck speed that characterizes broadcast and online media reporting, waiting to hear from slower—even if perhaps more reliable—sources might not be politically feasible.

Although media often seem to drive events, when it comes to citizens' political action the role that media play should not be exalted to the point at which the courage of individuals is underrated. Despite the rush in 2011 to define the uprisings in the Middle East as "the Facebook revolution" or "the Twitter revolution," these movements belonged to people, not to media, and to characterize them otherwise is to insult those who took the risk to go into the streets to demand change.

Media are just tools; nothing more. Whether the carbon copies of samizdat writings that were circulated surreptitiously in the Soviet Union or the YouTube videos that were produced by young Egyptians, media manifestations of resistance and rebellion can inform and encourage, but the actions that bring about change must be undertaken by individuals, and lasting change requires reform, and sometimes rebirth, of institutions.

Those are general principles that should be kept in mind when evaluating the relationship between media and diplomacy, and when analyzing the role of media in events such as the Arab revolutions. Beyond these broad concepts are specific cases drawn from a long history of the interaction between media and international affairs.

★   ★   ★

This book examines three major topics: the Arab revolutions of 2011; the altered theories and practices of diplomacy necessitated by the new pace and reach of information flow; and the ways social media-based networks affect political structure and activism.

The events of 2011 in the Arab world offer an intriguing perspective on twenty-first-century politics. The uprisings that began in Tunisia were not spontaneous in the sense that they arose from nothing. The political foundation of revolution is not built that way. The grievances, frustrations, and anger about the economic and social status quo in most Arab states had been growing for decades. The trigger for revolt was the suicide by self-immolation of Mohamed Bouazizi in Sidi Bouzid, Tunisia. He was a former college student who, like many others, could not find a better job than selling fruits and vegetables on the city streets. In despair about his future and after being harassed by police, he set himself on fire in December 2010 and died the following month.

Bouazizi's death triggered the revolt in Tunisia, serving as a "last straw" for thousands of Tunisians who saw in his frustration a mirror-image of their own lives. Social media were the initial amplifiers of this frustration. Facebook became the town square—a relatively protected zone where dissent could be expressed to a largely sympathetic audience without the same level of fear of the state security apparatus that might have muted protests in physical, rather than cyber, space.

Given the limited Internet access in Tunisia, the protest movement was provided a huge lift by an older medium: television. Satellite channels, particularly Qatar-based Al Jazeera, aggregated material from Facebook, YouTube, and other online sources and broadcast it to a vast audience. In Tunisia, broadband penetration is just 24 percent, but television penetration is 93 percent,[1] which underscores the significance of television channels as sometimes the most far-reaching disseminators of social media content.

A word should also be said about even older media—print and radio. In much of the world, these are still the best ways to reach the many people, especially in rural areas, who have little or no access to television or Internet-based sources. Radio has special value to those who cannot read or write.

As historian Robert Darnton noted, "The marvels of communication technology in the present have produced a false consciousness about the past—even a sense that communication has no history, or had nothing of importance to consider before the days of television and the Internet."[2] Darnton pointed out: "Radio did not destroy the newspaper; television did not kill radio; and the Internet did not make TV extinct. In each case the information environment became richer and more complex. That is what we are experiencing in this crucial phase of transition to a dominantly digital ecology."[3]

To cite just two oft-cited examples of "old media's" clout, William Randolph Hearst's incendiary newspaper headlines in 1898 helped create the Spanish American War, and Edward R. Murrow's radio broadcasts from London in 1940 helped change the course of World War II by building American support for intervention.

Every unhappy country is unhappy in its own way, and so the stories of the Arab states' upheavals vary. Some leaders, such as King Abdullah in Jordan and Morocco's King Mohammed, proved agile enough to survive the initial surge of emotion in the region. In Tunisia and Egypt, the army made clear that it would not go to war against its fellow citizens. In Libya, however, chaos prevailed as events reflected the vicious lunacy of that country's leader, Muammar Qaddafi. As this book is written, the future of regimes in Yemen, Bahrain, Algeria, and Syria remain uncertain, and even the Saudi monarchy nervously attempts to ensure its survival by long overdue spending to improve the lives of Saudis who do not happen to be members of the royal family. One of the oddities of 2011 was that Lebanon, scene of such persistent turmoil over the years, suddenly seemed one of the most stable countries in the region.

In addition to the internal dynamics of individual states, new interregional relationships—some quite tense—took shape. Saudi troops and United Arab Emirates police entered Bahrain to bolster the royal family there. The Saudis carefully strengthened their southern frontier forces as Yemen's government teetered toward implosion. Outside powers meddled: Iran was presumed to be encouraging Shia opposition groups in Bahrain and elsewhere, and the United States and other NATO countries committed their firepower to aid the Libyan insurrection. Turkey scolded Syria, Libya, and Israel, and Israel itself held on nervously as tremors shook its fragile relationships with its neighbors.

If this scenario had been suggested just six months earlier, even the most avid devotee of fictional thrillers would have rejected the story line as implausible. So, governments might argue that they should be excused for not having contingency plans prepared for such unlikely events. But they deserve little sympathy; their failures cannot simply be attributed to cloudy crystal balls. Governments around the world were caught unaware because they did not understand how media were changing national and global political dynamics by empowering citizens to the point at which they could do something about the circumstances that were making their lives miserable.

Diplomats who claim to be up to date because they have their own Twitter accounts or Facebook pages miss the point. Many of them are enamored of gadgetry without recognizing what media tools can really do on a macro level. The foreign policy establishment in many countries is exceedingly slow to recognize change, in this case the impact of networks that communication-based connectivity enables.

Some of the major powers still seem enamored of strategies that worked well during the cold war. Perhaps, in retrospect, those appear to have been desirably simpler days, with the principal adversaries clearly identified and the rest of the world's nations serving as supporting players that could be courted or ignored, depending on the superpowers' whims. The information space could be defined and controlled; propaganda could be delivered to audiences with few alternative sources of news about the world.

Today the cold war's trickle of information has become a torrent, and navigating the flow requires a sturdy craft that has been designed to sustain the buffeting that is part of the new strategic information environment. This book will address ways that diplomacy and broader political mechanisms are affected by this, and will suggest changes that might help lift governments' work into realistic modernity.

Part of this revision of practice will require a thoughtful appraisal of social media's power. Wael Ghonim, a Google executive who was a major player in the Tahrir Square protests, said that the revolution began "in June 2010 when hundreds of thousands of Egyptians started collaborating content. We would post a video on Facebook that would be shared by 60,000 people on their walls within a few hours. I've always said that if you want to liberate a society, just give them the Internet."[4]

That pronouncement, and others like it, was a product of the euphoria surrounding the fall of Hosni Mubarak, and it should be taken as such. Just giving people the Internet does not guarantee a revolution, certainly not a successful one. A different view was expressed by journalist Richard Engel, who said of events in Egypt: "This didn't have anything to do with Twitter and Facebook. This had to do with people's dignity, people's pride. People are not able to feed their families."[5]

A case can also be made that the events of 2011 were not true "revolutions" because a revolution requires substantive institutional restructuring, not just regime change. As David and Marina Ottaway observed, the prodemocracy activists in Tunisia and Egypt "have not brought to the fore a new ruling class, a system of governance, or the profound social and economic changes associated with the classical meaning of revolution. And it remains to be seen whether they will succeed in doing so."[6]

Nevertheless, whatever term is used to describe events in the Arab world in 2011, it can be said that these were the most important changes in international affairs since the collapse of European communism in 1989. Most foreign policy experts, in and out of government, were surprised by the speed and breadth of events, and some soon recognized that diplomacy will require imaginative restructuring if it is to deal effectively with such events in the future.

This book offers some historical background about how the cushion of time that diplomats once enjoyed has steadily diminished. The shrinking accelerated during the past half-century, driven at first by the growing influence of television. Internet-based media have changed the nature of information flow in ways that have further necessitated rapid-reaction diplomacy.

In diplomacy as in other aspects of public policy, responding quickly and responding wisely might be very different. Traditional diplomats from the George Kennan or Dean Acheson school would presumably argue that diplomacy and speed are not only incompatible, but they are fundamentally antithetical. But today's world requires rapid response; the public expects it and political changes are fueled by high-speed communication that causes them to zoom past careful diplomats. Good diplomatic practice should not be tossed aside, but it must adapt to the pace of events more comprehensively than it has to date.

Part of this change in the practice of diplomacy must take place in the field, where diplomats should develop better contacts with the general population than they do today. Former US undersecretary of state Marc Grossman has described an "expeditionary diplomat" who breaks free from the isolation of working behind embassy walls and contacting just a narrow array of host-country officials. This new approach has its risks, personal security among them, but it also has significant potential benefits.

Such expeditionary diplomacy would be part of a greater emphasis on public diplomacy. Working with publics, not just governments, is particularly important now that communications technologies have empowered individuals in terms of their ability to access information and connect with one another. More than ever before, they can learn about the larger world. For too long, public diplomacy has been looked on by some as being a "nice" but nonessential exercise that supplements traditional, manipulative propaganda efforts. If that was ever true, it certainly is not the case now. As the events of 2011 illustrate, power *can* emanate from the public, and so developing and maintaining ties with publics around the world is an essential element of foreign policy.

Doing so will require more resources than most countries make available today, and, more important, it means making public diplomacy much more central in the creation and implementation of foreign policy. This will involve more than devising new titles for officials and expanding staff numbers. It will require remapping the terrain of international relations, with traditional state-to-state linkages being enlarged to incorporate far more state-to-people programs than now exist and to make them much more integral in a nation's diplomacy.

One of the factors behind these needed changes is the same technology that was so visible during the 2011 revolutions, social media. These participatory media forms include the well-known Facebook, Twitter, and YouTube, as well as many variations, with new ones popping up almost every day. An introductory explanation of the significance of these media is this: Consider the traditional ways to get information—the newspaper that arrives on your doorstep when the newspaper company decides to deliver it; the television newscast that appears on your screen when the broadcast company decides to present it. In these and similar cases there were distinct providers and consumers of content. The consumers were passive recipients, selecting items from a very limited menu of offerings. They had choices, the numbers of which rose and fell as newspapers (especially those delivered in the evening) closed and television channels grew, but the public had little ability to be providers themselves except in limited ways, such as through writing letters or talking face-to-face or on the telephone.

Within the past few years, all this has changed. Almost anyone can both gather and disseminate information. The most widespread tool for this is the mobile telephone; more than 5 billion were in use worldwide by mid-2010.[7] Record a few minutes of video on your phone, post it on YouTube, and millions can watch whatever *you* have decided is newsworthy. For many, such "news" consists of the cute antics of a child, but others, such as those who recorded images of upheaval in Sanaa or Damascus, become independent, one-person news suppliers—"journalists" in a broad sense of the word.

Beyond dissemination of information, these social media tools provide infrastructure for networks that in a political context can be the foundation of a revolutionary movement. Or so the argument goes. Critics argue that social media-based networks are flimsy because they are too easy to join, regardless of the joiner's motivation. Malcolm Gladwell wrote: "The platforms of social media are built around weak ties. Twitter is a way of following (or being followed by) people you may never have met. Facebook is a tool for efficiently managing your acquaintances, for keeping up with people you would not otherwise be able to stay in touch with. That's why you can have a thousand 'friends' on Facebook, as you never could in real life.... Social networks are effective at increasing *participation*—by lessening the level of motivation that participation requires."[8]

Clay Shirky viewed social media as more significant: "Do social media allow insurgents to adopt new strategies? And have those strategies ever been crucial? Here, the historical record of the last decade is unambiguous: yes, and yes. Digital networks have acted as a massive positive supply shock to the cost and spread of information, to the ease and range of public speech by citizens, and to the speed and scale of group coordination."[9]

This debate shows no signs of abating, and this book provides fuel for both sides. Social media have certainly been influential in the shift toward citizen power, but *how* influential—whether they play a truly determinative role—in events such as the Arab revolutions is worth exploring.

At issue is not just the function of social media in themselves, but the displacement of traditional hierarchies by networks. This is more than a semantic issue, because diplomacy and other political mechanisms will need to be realigned to deal with the rise of networks. The stratified structures of leadership common in most states will not disappear overnight, but the dispersed elements of networks will become more significant as the newest communication technologies become more widespread, fostering increased connectivity among these elements.

A foremost scholar of networks, Manuel Castells, defines networks as "complex structures of communication constructed around a set of goals that simultaneously ensure unity of purpose and flexibility of execution by their adaptability to the operating environment.... Their structure evolves according to the capacity of the network to self-configure in an endless search for more efficient networking arrangements."[10]

Castells adds that "networks became the most efficient organizational forms as a result of three major features of networks which benefitted from the new technological environment: flexibility, scalability, and survivability. Flexibility is the ability to reconfigure according to changing environments and retain their goals while changing their components, sometimes bypassing blocking points of communication channels to find new connections. Scalability is the ability to expand or shrink with little disruption. Survivability is the ability of networks, because they have no single center and can operate in a wide range of configurations, to withstand attacks..."[11]

The ability to reconfigure is the key to decentralized networks' effectiveness in contexts such as those of the 2011 Arab uprisings. In many cases, a traditional hierarchic structure lacks the agility to avoid fast and ferocious suppression by established forces of power, and does not possess networks' communication orientation. (Some scholars argue that hierarchies are an older form of networks—and that hierarchies can themselves be nodes in networks.) The adaptability of networks also adds levels of complexity to diplomacy because networks' protean nature can disrupt the consistency on which diplomats prefer to rely.

Given networks' flexibility and their interconnected but dispersed nodes, social media are useful tools in providing cohesion within the network. They are well suited for providing the non-linear communication apparatus that network participants require. Networked forms of organization predate social media networks, but social media networks often mirror existing networks and make ties within them more efficient in times of crisis.

In evaluating the significance of social media in a networked society, it is important to avoid absolutist pronouncements about the extent to which these media have transformed the public sphere. They are very important—there is no doubt about that—but are they truly transformative in themselves? This book argues that they are not, that the transformation of political life as seen during the Arab revolutions arose from more traditional issues related to economic welfare, oppressive government behavior, and the overall miserable kind of life forced upon millions of people by autocratic regimes.

There is nothing intrinsically modern about any of this. Read a history of events leading up to America's revolution and the parallels are striking. Symbolic acts of resistance, such as the Boston Tea Party, led to increasingly fierce confrontations with distant leaders and their deputies who at first refused to entertain the notion of freedom for those they ruled. Rebellious colonists operated through networks well before the concept of a "United States" took hold. The Americans found that armed conflict was the only way to secure their desired ends, and it was not until the American victory at the Battle of Yorktown in 1781 that the independence proclaimed in 1776 was assured. The length and bitterness of this struggle may foreshadow challenges to be faced in some Arab states during the coming years.

Nevertheless, hope should remain intact. Although it is stated with eloquence that now may seem archaic to some, the final passage of the Declaration of Independence would ring true among many of today's Arab revolutionaries: "We mutually pledge to each other our lives, our fortunes, and our sacred honor."

★　★　★

Reflecting on the past is always useful, but the pressures of modernity are the principal factors reshaping diplomacy today. This book was born partly because of the uproar about the allegedly slow response of the outside world to the fast-accelerating events in the Arab states during 2011. In evaluating such criticism, a question arises: How can any policymaker keep up with the vast amount of information coming from a vast number of sources?

The public's expectations are geared to the speed of the information flow, but that does not necessarily mean that those who govern should try to match their policy implementation to the pace of this flow. Fast policymaking is often unwise policymaking, but that is an inadequate answer to those who are accustomed to getting their news with the click of a mouse and expect to see crises resolved by the next time they click. This book does not endorse trying to match the pace of diplomacy to the speed of social and other media, but it does suggest that policymakers must do a better job of addressing the political realities and technological capabilities of a social media-oriented society that relies heavily on networks of various kinds to acquire the information used in decision making and political action.

Although no precise how-to-do formula emerges from considering these matters, this book may help establish the context in which policymakers and the public will be considering and responding to political events for years to come. The Arab Awakening of 2011 is just a starting point, and a long path lies ahead.

PART I

2011

CHAPTER 1

THE POLITICAL REVOLUTION

On August 2, 2011, these were the headlines on the Al Jazeera English website:

- "Mubarak on Trial"
- "The Battle for Libya"
- "Syria Uprising"
- "Yemen Unrest"

Amazing.

The day-by-day, and sometimes minute-by-minute, descriptions of events in the Arab world during 2011 constitute a thrilling story that will engross policymakers, journalists, historians, and perhaps filmmakers for years to come.

Following the resignation of Egypt's president Hosni Mubarak on February 11, 2011, President Barack Obama said: "There are very few moments in our lives when we have the privilege to witness history taking place. This is one of those moments." Obama added, "Over the past few weeks, the wheel of history turned at a blinding pace."[1] When the wheel of history spins so quickly, policymakers need to keep up with it, and policy is rarely formulated wisely "at a blinding pace."

These historic developments may also affect the futures of people and institutions far removed from the events of the moment. What happened in Egypt in 2011 might well have ramifications in Zimbabwe in 2013 or China in 2015. And the Arab Awakening will certainly affect the way governments around the world deal with each other and with different publics—their own citizens and those of other nations. Those who hold power take note of such consequential tremors.

The uprisings of 2011 happened to take place in Arab states, but they represent a change in the world order that is more generational than geographical or cultural. People born during the last few decades of the twentieth century constitute the first truly global generation. New information and communication technologies connect them to each other regardless of physical distance or political obstruction. Young persons in a Moroccan village can watch Al Jazeera and see what is happening at that instant in Egypt. Then they can send text messages (or, if the technology is available, Tweets) to let others know what has just occurred and what they might do in response. They can build a community on Facebook and scour the Web for information about political tactics they wish to employ. This generation's access to the rest of the world is much different from the relative isolation their parents knew, when information flow was limited by lower-tech tools and controlled by governments.

Some of those who govern still try to obstruct these new modes of information distribution, and they will be able to succeed for a while. The Iranian oligarchy slows Internet speed to impair video downloading. China's government monitors online communication of various kinds. Egypt's Mubarak regime, in its final spasms, shut down the Internet. None of this will work, at least not for long. Unless you are a government such as North Korea's, which doesn't mind cutting itself off from the rest of the world, restricting communication for political purposes is almost certain to bring economic ruin. No one will do business with you without Internet access. And any attempt to block online traffic inspires the geeks of the world—some of them funded by intelligence agencies—to find ways to bypass cyber obstacles.

Information *will* reach people, and when it does, it will—in many cases—prove to be liberating and empowering. Even more so is the ability to disseminate that information. The communication-based networks of shared interests that have evolved in recent years are powered by information for which there is growing hunger. Some of these networks are used for destructive purposes, such as those created by Al Qaeda and similar groups. But many more are helping to bring about constructive change through democratic mobilization.

This new Arab generation challenged the repression their countries had known for so long. In some cases, they achieved success with incredible speed. In others, those who held power pushed back fiercely, thwarting—or perhaps just delaying—political and social reforms. Other countries were at first just bystanders, but then nervously edged into the events unfolding before them.

That the entire region was affected had immediate ramifications elsewhere. The Arab world, with its oil and natural gas, is a critical part of the global economy's foundation. The region's relationship with its neighbors has complex strategic ramifications for matters ranging from Israel's existence to immigration into Western Europe. Although it comprises only about 20 percent of the world's Muslim population, the Arab world is the heart of Islam and so events there reverberate throughout the *ummah,* the global Muslim community.

So, this great awakening must be taken seriously. It all began during the final days of 2010, when a young Tunisian decided that he had endured injustice for long enough.

Tunisia

Mohamed Bouazizi was a former university student trying to eke out a living for himself and his family by selling fruits and vegetables on the streets of Sidi Bouzid, a city of about 40,000 in central Tunisia. His weighing scales, essential tools of his business, were confiscated by authorities, presumably because he had not paid the bribes local officials demanded. After a confrontation with a city inspector, Bouazizi went to the governor's office to protest, but was turned away. He returned, with his cart, to the governor's office, and shouted, "How do you expect me to earn a living?" and poured paint thinner over himself. Then he lit a match.

While Bouazizi was hospitalized with third-degree burns over 90 percent of his body, his mother, other family members, and friends went to the governor's office and threw coins at the fence surrounding it, yelling, "Here is your bribe." Bouazizi's cousin posted the video of the protest on YouTube, and soon Al Jazeera and other channels outside the control of the Tunisian government telecast it. Reports were also posted on Facebook and Twitter.[2]

About a third of Tunisia's 10 million citizens use the Internet, and Facebook is particularly popular there, with more than 2 million users.[3] This relatively high level of access to Web-based information plus the even greater pervasiveness of television meant that people throughout Tunisia quickly became aware of the Bouazizi case, and when the young street vendor died on January 4, 2011, demonstrations throughout the country grew more intense.

On January 13, Tunisian president Zine el-Abidine Ben Ali made a desperate appeal to his angry nation. He had ruled without significant challenge since 1987, but he now admitted the need for "deep and comprehensive change," and said, "I have understood you." He promised to allow media freedom and to reduce prices of basic food items, and he pledged that he would step down in 2014—"No presidency for life."[4]

None of this slowed the protests, and Tunisian military commanders told the president that they would not use force against demonstrators. On January 14, the day after his speech, Ben Ali fled to Saudi Arabia and Tunisia began to rebuild itself. The interim government that replaced Ben Ali was seen by the public as just a continuation of the old regime, and a "second revolution" picked up where the first had left off. In early March, the titular president, Fouad Mebazaa, announced that the government would agree to all the protestors' demands. He said that a "national constituent assembly" would be elected and it would rewrite Tunisia's constitution, serving as "a mirror that truly reflects the people's ambitions." He added, "We announce the beginning of a new era based upon the full rule of the people over a new political system that definitively breaks with the old regime."[5]

Root Causes

Tunisia's uprising was the spark that ignited much of the Arab world, but the roots of this rebellion ran far deeper than the martyrdom of Mohamed Bouazizi. The fundamental relationship between the government and the people was badly skewed. Michele Penner Angrist observed that "the Ben Ali regime was contemptuous of its citizens, treating them as too unsophisticated to entrust with freedoms—and betting that they would be too meek to call the regime to account for its excesses."[6] This nasty condescension was a characteristic of most Arab governments. Also, despite Tunisia's relatively high levels of literacy and middle-class stability, it suffered from the kinds of decay that were festering throughout the region. Marc Lynch cited "a combination of authoritarian retrenchment, unfulfilled economic promises, rising sectarianism at the popular level, and deep frustration among an increasingly tech-savvy rising generation."[7]

In the aspirations and discontent of that rising generation can be found the driving force behind the Arab revolutions, which Ben Ali and other Arab autocrats underestimated. Almost a third of the Arab population is between the ages of 15 and 29. More than any preceding generation, they are connected to the larger world. Through YouTube, websites, and other new tech venues, they can see the progress of others of their age group around the globe, and they compare this to the relative lack of progress they themselves are making. Young people connect with one another, within their own countries and far beyond, and this gives them confidence to act; they know that they are not alone.

Whichever Arab country they live in, many in this age group have at least one thing in common—they cannot find a job. The youth unemployment rate in the region is about 24 percent, and in certain places it is much higher. This is nothing new, but more and more of these young jobless men and women have college degrees. Regimes in the region made college more accessible as a short-term fix for the job shortage, but the main result of this is that now the *hittistes*—French-Arabic slang for those who lean against walls with nothing else to do—are increasingly well educated, and are frustrated by the lack of jobs. In Tunisia in 1990 only about 2 percent of people over age 15 had postsecondary degrees, but by 2010 the number was 6.7 percent, and yet employment prospects were no less bleak.[8] A 2010 Gallup survey found that more than a quarter of all young people in Arab countries wanted to emigrate, with the figure reaching 40 percent in Tunisia and Yemen.[9]

These numbers reflect the hopelessness that may eventually turn to anger and produce political upheaval, wherever the situation exists, whether in an Arab country or in India, Turkey, the United Kingdom, or other countries where young people see a dismal future in front of them. For those who can find jobs, labor unions may become increasingly significant as mechanisms that provide channels for political frustration. In Tunisia, where the labor movement was well established, workers kept the heat on Ben Ali's immediate successors and helped sustain the "second revolution" from which lasting substantive change may yet emerge.

The United States inadvertently provided further impetus for reform through the contents of diplomatic documents made public by WikiLeaks. Among the documents was a cable from the US ambassador to Tunisia reporting that half the members of the country's commercial elite were directly related to President Ben Ali. This message and other critical commentary provided no surprises to Tunisians, but the scathing comments in the WikiLeaks papers indicated that US support for Ben Ali would be minimal. Perhaps more significant was the embarrassment produced by such appraisals from a foreign power. The shame of being considered a criminal state gave anti-regime Tunisians a further rationale for taking action.[10]

Recognizing the political and economic roots of the Arab uprisings eliminates some of the romanticized notions about the process of revolution. Spontaneity plays little part in successful uprisings that are the products of deep-rooted problems. The anger that drives people toward courageous action has built up over years, or even generations, and it is anger grounded in the basics of life: having a decent place to live; being able to find a stable job; putting food on the kitchen table. When a government allows those elements of daily life to become unattainable, revolution seems a tantalizing remedy and, given enough time and the right circumstances, an inevitable outcome.

Such conditions have long been at the root of revolution, but a principal difference today is the interactivity that is part of political upheaval. If you are without a job, you can go onto Facebook and find others in similar circumstances. If you see police breaking up a demonstration, you can use Twitter to instantly let others know what is happening, and you can post the video of the brawl on YouTube. The impact of the content posted on all such venues then can be greatly magnified if international television news organizations such as Al Jazeera aggregate the material individuals have posted and deliver it to their tens of millions of viewers.

As all this is happening, governments outside the region are (or should be) monitoring the information, trying to sort the important from the unimportant, the true from the untrue, and then deciding if and how to respond. This process is expected to move swiftly, matching the pace of the information flow.

Meanwhile, other societal forces come into play. In the Middle East, religion is one of the most significant.

Islam

The Arab Spring of 2011 was not the conservative Muslim uprising that some in the West had fearfully anticipated. Given the overwhelmingly Muslim populations of Arab countries (e.g., 97 percent in Tunisia, 90 percent in Egypt) and the activism of Islamists in the region, the relatively secular nature of the Arab Awakening—at least in its early stages—is striking.

"Islamism" is politicized Islam, and its variations range from a firm commitment to democracy to the violent intolerance of the so-called jihadis who claim that their vicious pursuits are prescribed by the Holy Qur'an.

There might not be a full-blown "clash of civilizations" between the West and Islam, but there certainly is an abundance of misunderstanding. "Jihad" is an example of sloppy interpretation creating significant misperceptions. The word can be translated as "to exert" and "to strive" as well as "to battle," and even "battling" translation does not necessarily involve warfare, but rather the battle against personal failings. Many Muslims consider jihad as a path to self-improvement in one's relationship with Allah, and as part of this fully reject violence.

Nevertheless, in the West, the most pejorative meaning seems to have taken hold as the most commonly used. Based on that, Robin Wright has described a "counterjihad" in the Muslim world, the goal of which is "to rout extremism in its many forms" and "to rescue Islam's central values from a small but virulent minority." Wright adds that "politically, the counter-jihad craves changes compatible with a globalizing world and basic rights for the faithful. But it rejects strict secularism and Westernization. The quest is more about 'just values'—equitable justice for all, political participation for all, free speech for all, and rights of self-determination for all—adapted to Muslim societies." Wright cited the view of newspaper editor Khaled al Maeena, who said, "Every mother in Saudi Arabia or any other Gulf country wants her son or daughter to carry a laptop rather than a rifle or a dagger. The appeal of death and destruction doesn't carry much significance anymore because the jihadis have failed to provide anything constructive."[11]

This does not mean that those with a more rigid view of Islam have permanently stepped aside. In late July 2011, hundreds of thousands of Islamists gathered in Cairo's Tahrir Square to claim the Egyptian revolution as their own and to demand that Egypt adopt strict *sharia* law as the foundation of its postrevolution society. Also in Egypt, right-wing Salafi Muslims were reported to be instigators of lethal attacks against Coptic Christians, and Salafis fared well in the first round of parliamentary voting in late 2011. In such circumstances, the less-well-organized moderates tried to decide how to present their own case. It was a difficult task; they did not want to back away from their religion, but they were determined not to allow the revolution they had engineered to be captured by intolerant radicals. But at least for the time being, they found themselves overmatched by the conservatives, who were able to rely on the Muslim Brotherhood's well-established political apparatus. Many of those who dismissed predictions of conflict between the Muslim and non-Muslim world as overwrought now saw in the angry aspects of the Arab Spring evidence that a struggle would occur, but mainly within Islam.

Another example of this tension could be seen in Morocco in the aftermath of the turmoil in Egypt. King Mohammed VI proposed a series of reforms that would have the monarch share certain duties with the prime minister and other councillors, while the king retains almost all the most significant authority. A clause in the proposed new constitution called for "freedom of faith," which the Islamic-oriented Justice and Development Party immediately criticized as challenging the primacy of Islam and opening the door to conversions to Christianity and other religions. The constitutional provision was revised to state that Islam is the "religion of state which guarantees to all the free exercise of religion."[12] That is the kind of domestic diplomacy that is necessary in order to ensure compatibility between religion and reform.

Of course, no one knows with any certainty how all this will play out, but in the Arab states the connection between Islam and politics is strong. A survey conducted by the Pew Research Center during spring 2010 in Egypt found that while only 48 percent of respondents said that Islam played a large role in their country's politics,

85 percent said that Islam's influence in politics is positive, while only 2 percent said the influence was negative. (In two non-Arab countries with large Muslim populations, the survey found Islam to be an even stronger force. In Indonesia, 89 percent of Muslims said Islam played a large role and 91 percent thought it was a positive influence. Among Nigerian Muslims, 88 percent said Islam played a large role, and 82 percent said it was positive.) In Egypt, 20 percent of respondents said they were "very concerned" about Islamic extremism, while 41 percent said they were "somewhat concerned." Also in Egypt, 31 percent of those surveyed said they perceived an ongoing struggle between modernizers and fundamentalists. These respondents identified with fundamentalists rather than with modernizers by 59 to 27 percent.[13]

Governments such as those of the United States and other Western nations always seem behind the curve when dealing with religion as an element of foreign policy. In the United States, the constitutionally required separation of church and state makes policymakers squeamish about dealing with religious matters, even when it is someone else's religion and country that are at issue. Approaching religion-related issues gingerly will not work in relationships with Arab countries in which religion and government are inextricably connected. (Among non-Arab Muslim states, Iran's governance structure is another version of this connection.)

Anyone who has spent time in the Arab world recognizes the significance of religion in the ambiance of daily life and in the conceptualization of politics: for example, the muezzin's call to prayer, the frequent use in conversation of *insh'allah* (God willing), the conservative clothing worn by many. This ubiquity of religion may seem strange to Westerners, but without comprehending its importance there is no way to understand society and politics in predominantly Muslim states. That the Qur'an is God's word and that the Prophet Mohammed is God's messenger are not debatable matters; the dominant politics as well as faith of the region are deeply rooted in this. Whatever their own feelings about this, policymakers from other countries must appreciate the importance of religion as the center of life for many Arabs.

An entire Islamic media culture exists in Arabic and other languages. It can provide outsiders—including policymakers—with valuable insights about background issues and real-time events. The preeminent satellite channel, Al Jazeera, has some overtly religious content, such as the program *Sharia and Life* presented by the cleric Yusef al-Qaradawi, who in addition to commanding a global television audience is a leading figure in Egypt's religious and political affairs. Long at odds with the Mubarak regime, al-Qaradawi returned to Egypt after Mubarak's fall and became a magnet for conservative religionists while supporting the changes in the country. He spoke at Tahrir Square on February 23, 2011, and delivered a message that was in part nonreligious: "We inevitably must be patient a little longer. I call on everyone who has stopped working, or is striking, or is sitting-in, to contribute to this revolution with his work. Egypt wants you to work. The Egyptian economy is underdeveloped and it is not permitted to us who supported the revolution to be a cause of retarding the construction of Egypt."[14]

In addition to the major satellite news organizations, religious satellite channels proliferate in the Arab world, as do Islamic websites. Even nontraditional Islamic preachers, such as Amr Khaled, trained as an accountant rather than a theologian, have tremendous media-based followings, especially among young audiences both within the Arab states and in the Muslim diaspora. Favoring European suits and polo shirts rather than a cleric's robes, Khaled relies on Western vernacular, as when he talks about Islam "empowering" women, and describes Prophet Mohammed as "the first manager." His website is one of the most popular Arabic sites and is translated into 16 other languages, and his videos help attract a wider audience. As of fall 2011, Khaled had 3.45 million Facebook "likes" and more than 178,000 Twitter followers.[15]

He tells women that they must wear the *hijab*, but—unlike al-Qaradawi—he does not often offer opinions on matters such as whether people should join the Palestinian resistance. His principal themes include fostering an Arab and Islamic revival by increasing literacy and community involvement. When addressing European Muslims, he stresses the importance of coexistence—for those living in the United Kingdom, he recommends rooting for a British soccer team, not Pakistan's; and for those in France, he supports lobbying for the legal right to wear the *hijab* in school, while, in the meantime, making do with designer hats.[16]

Khaled's message is usually not overtly political, but it provides insight into the social and political environment of Arab Muslims.

He began a television show called *Tomorrow Is Better* in May 2011, broadcasting from the streets of Cairo, rather than from a studio. He is adept at reading the political mood, particularly among younger people. He told an interviewer that in 2006 he asked his followers to tell him what they wanted to see in their lives 20 years in the future. He reported receiving 1.4 million replies and said the number one response was, "We want and need jobs."[17]

Khaled has personal political aspirations, and his sharp political instincts make him worth watching. He told an interviewer in early 2011: "I believe I have had a political role since I started, to make the civil society more active. Now I think that I have a deeper role in political issues. But in the right time. With the right image. I'll go to this role for sure, but step by step in the right way."[18]

In the West, the political impact of TV preachers such as Pat Robertson tended to dissipate quickly once they entered mainstream politics, but a strong case can be made that those who shape policy related to the Arab world would be wise to pay close attention to Qaradawi, Khaled, and other religious leaders. Doing so would be part of recognizing that the relationship between Islam and Arab society and politics is very different from the political-religious relationships in most of the West.

The generational difference between the two men is reflected in their respective online presences. Kahled has a strong Twitter and Facebook presence, but Qaradawi has a Twitter account in his name, with no Tweets and slightly more than 400 followers, and on Facebook, Qaradawi has fewer than 300,000 friends. As for websites, Qaradawi's presence is mostly limited to brief videos, while Khaled, according to John Esposito, "uses his website interactively to mobilize as well as instruct," and he draws a large response from those who follow him on line.[19]

Qaradawi and Khaled are just two religious-media personalities among many whose public pronouncements may have political ramifications and, therefore, are worth scrutinizing. This open-source intelligence can be valuable in evaluating the attitudes of Arab publics and so serve as background information for policymakers. Understanding Islam is not wholly a theological matter, but rather involves recognizing political and other characteristics of Arab society and how they are affected by religion. In Saudi Arabia, where governance is most tightly linked to Islam, or in Lebanon, where the ties, at least for some political leaders, are much looser, assessments of the role of Islam will vary considerably. If policymakers are to respond promptly to events in this region, those assessments must be constantly updated, and media monitoring is one part of the foundation for doing so.

Among religious-political organizations, the Muslim Brotherhood is the best established in the Arab states. Founded in Egypt in 1928 by Hassan al-Banna (1906–1949), it has been influenced strongly by the conservative teachings of Sayyid Qutb (1906–1966), an intellectual who became a militant after being jailed and tortured by the Egyptian government. The most radical of Muslim Brotherhood activists advocate using any means necessary to defend Islam against what they see as subversion by the West and by secular influences within Arab states. More mainstream members consider the Brotherhood to be a fundamentally moderate political organization, seeking reforms based on the teachings of Islam. The Brotherhood, which favors segregation of the sexes (although it has a growing number of women members), tries to present a nonthreatening profile to the global public, even featuring an English-language website (www.ikhwanweb.com). Its political presence takes shape in the form of the Freedom and Justice Party in Egypt, Hamas in Palestine, and more generally in endorsements of political reform.

The Brotherhood did not play a leading role in the initial stages of the Arab Awakening of 2011, lending support belatedly to anti-government demonstrators in Egypt. There were two principal reasons behind this caution: if the uprising failed, the government would have a good excuse for intensifying its repression of the Brothers; and the Brothers' involvement would allow the protestors' opponents to slap the label "Islamist" on the revolution. On the other hand, if the uprising succeeded, the Brotherhood would be seen as irrelevant if it had not participated. Indecision led to a split within the organization, as younger members were much more inclined to actively support the protests, while the old-guard Brothers remained on the sidelines. By the end of January, however, the Brotherhood threw its support behind the revolution it had not helped to create.[20]

This generational divide became pronounced within the Brotherhood in 2011, with some of the group's younger members eagerly embracing technology-based organizing and willingness to assist non-Brotherhood demonstrations. The older, hard-line Brothers were more reluctant to go beyond the Brotherhood's own boundaries. The debate within the organization was articulated several years before, when Ibrahim Hodeibi, a younger Brotherhood member and a blogger, suggested that the Brotherhood credo, "Islam is the answer," should give way to "Egypt for all Egyptians."[21] This more secular slogan was not adopted by the Brotherhood, but at some point Islamism and nationalism will need to be reconciled.

Western policymakers tend to have a reflexive negative response to any mention of the Muslim Brotherhood. The organization has enough extremist influences within it to make this wariness sensible, but the Brothers are so pervasively organized within much of the Arab world that they need to be dealt with at some level. Their existence was long used by Mubarak as a rationale for not opening up Egypt's political system, and the West did not challenge this in any meaningful way.

Now, according to Shadi Hamid, "what comes next may be the Arab world's first sustained experiment in Islamist integration."[22] The non-Muslim world's policymakers would be foolish to write off this experiment without giving it a chance and watching it closely.

★   ★   ★

As the role of Islam takes shape in the changed Arab states and various refinements in religion's role are considered, Turkey is sometimes cited as a state with certain aspects of national life that might lend themselves to adaptation in other progressive, predominantly Muslim countries. Turkey has created a defined space for Islam within a secular state, but, as the *Economist* noted, "Turkey's moderate Islamism did not evolve overnight. Its emergence, and taming, took a long time; it depended on many countervailing forces, including an army which was firm in its defense of a secular constitution and was strong enough, at least until recently, to deter any imposition of Islamic rule."[23] Turkey's unique status as a Muslim nation that is a member of NATO (North Atlantic Treaty Organization) and its emerging role as a regional leader—perhaps offsetting Iran's influence—make it an intriguing example of a different kind of role for Islam within a state. It is hard to imagine, however, any of the Arab countries moving very far in this direction unless an Arab version of Mustafa Kemal Ataturk were to come to the fore. At this time, that is highly unlikely.

★　★　★

The other politicoreligious issue that looms over the future of Arab politics is the role of Israel in the region. Western powers, especially the United States, have kept their distance from groups such as the Muslim Brotherhood because of these organizations' often virulent anti-Israel rhetoric. But Israel was not a factor in the Arab revolts of 2011. Aaron David Miller observed that "missing were the traditional anti-Zionist, anti-Semitic tropes, burning of Israeli and American flags, and demonstrations for Palestinian rights. None of this meant that the Arab world had given up the cause of Palestine, but it did reflect changing priorities, and a focus on domestic matters."[24] Even the attacks on the Israeli embassy in Cairo in September 2011 were sideshows, although such flare-ups make Israeli-Arab relations even more tenuous.

Despite not being a factor during the Arab Spring, Israel faces a time of unwelcome uncertainty. Will the new Egyptian government honor the Egypt-Israel peace treaty? What will be the relationships between new regimes in the region and Israel's principal foe, Iran? What will result from instability in Israel's contiguous neighbors, Syria and Jordan? The list of questions is endless.

No Arab government, old or new, will publicly abandon the Palestinians or embrace Israel. But as the political dynamics of the region undergo dramatic change, opportunities may present themselves for quiet diplomacy that alleviates long-term tensions, even if just a little bit. These opportunities might be short-lived, so real-time attentiveness by all parties will be crucial.

★　★　★

Changes in the Arab world rooted in the events of 2011 are not limited to politics. Archaic restrictions—legal and cultural—have long denied women the right to make decisions about their own lives and to play meaningful roles in building their society. Arab women, particularly younger Arab women, are fully aware that elsewhere in the world, women enjoy greater freedoms. As change comes to the awakened Arab countries, women do not intend to be left behind.

Women and the Arab Future

In July 2011, 60 Yemeni women came together to learn the intricacies of organizing, funding, and publicizing political campaigns. In the West, such gatherings are so common that they attract little attention. In Yemen, it was extraordinary, turning upside down the broadly accepted belief that women have no business involving themselves in public life. One of the organizers of the workshop, *Yemen Times* editor Nadia Al-Sakkaf, wrote, "It was amazing how the women, although they were from different political backgrounds and geographical locations, got together, fought, argued, agreed and moved ahead, so much unlike our Yemeni men who seem not to find in their heart the will or the ability to compromise."[25]

A significant by-product of the Arab Spring has been women's assertiveness as they participate in the newly energized political process. This promises to have long-lasting effect, altering the character of politics throughout much of the region. In most Arab countries, women's political involvement had taken the form of a few token appointments designed to advertise "progress" while ensuring that women remain virtually powerless. The Arab uprisings were chaotic enough to provide openings that women took advantage of, and by the time things began to settle down, women had established themselves to an unprecedented degree as contributors to building new political structures.

How long this lasts and where this leads are open to question. In Egypt, Bothaina Kamel, a television presenter and prodemocracy activist, became a candidate for president. Given little chance to win when she announced that she would run, she nevertheless underscored women's determination to not be shunted aside as they had been in the past.

At about the same time, a handful of women in Saudi Arabia were protesting prohibitions against their driving. Some of their protests—driving as long as they could before being stopped by police—were filmed and posted on YouTube so that other Arab women, and viewers around the world, could watch and applaud them.

As with many elements of the Arab Spring, the future role of women will be determined not by individuals in the limelight but rather by institutional change. Women have indicated that they expect to play a part in drafting new constitutions and political party rules to ensure removal of legal obstacles to their involvement. In general, their agenda is to ensure equal rights regarding education, employment, social advancement, and political participation.[26]

Women's identity and role in Arab society remains an issue that transcends politics. A barometer of change is the fluctuating popularity of the *hijab*, or headscarf. During the 1960s in Egypt, the headscarf was rarely seen, but in the half-century since then, it has made a comeback. Evidence of this can be found in college graduation photos; the percentage of women wearing the *hijab* appears to have increased significantly in recent decades. This is not necessarily a sign of women accepting disempowerment, but rather can be seen as an assertion of female religious identity. Harvard Divinity School professor Leila Ahmed wrote, "Where I once saw the veil as a symbol of intolerance, I now understand that for many women it is a badge of individuality and justice."[27]

As with many other indicators of change, attitudes about the *hijab* should be viewed as part of a larger portrait of societal transformation. Many policymakers outside the region are notorious for their lack of understanding of the Arab culture that is the foundation of politics. This is further complicated by the simplistic attitude that "an Arab is an Arab," which ignores the substantial differences among (and often within) the 22 countries that are members of the Arab League.

Also, different constituencies have different agendas, and the resulting tensions help shape events. In Egypt, for instance, the role of the military is far from certain. It did not intervene on behalf of the Mubarak regime, but how much democracy it will allow remains open to question. Dealing with such matters cannot be done merely by showing up periodically in Tahrir Square. Journalist Wendell Steavenson observed, "For intellectuals, drawn from the politicized elites, and for the bloggers and Facebook activists who instigated the protests, the challenge is to translate their revolutionary spirit into a genuine political force and to communicate their ideas to a wider population that remains generally conservative."[28]

Much the same can be said about the role of women during the transition to new forms of governance in the Arab states where change is taking hold. Women's rights and the exercise of those rights must be institutionalized or, as is the case with other reforms, they will soon wither and vanish.

Outsiders can be usefully supportive of this, but must be careful not to appear to be meddling. US secretary of state Hillary Rodham Clinton has been a persistent and effective champion of women's rights related to wide range of issues, and support from the United States and other Western nations for Arab women's progress has been helpful. Without introducing unwanted Westernizing influences, Clinton and others can support the development of women's organizations that will foster improved access to education, jobs, and participation in decisions that have an impact on diverse facets of society. The opening for this now exists.

Policymakers Awaken

"The people demand the removal of the regime."

That was the message—simple and direct—delivered by the protestors in Tunisia. Quickly, adroitly, and with the strength of their numbers, the activists got their wish: Ben Ali was gone and the prospect of building a new Tunisia was suddenly real.

For outsiders, this brief bit of democratic theater was a pleasant surprise. The audience applauded, promised support, and made ready to return to business as usual. Tunisia has little oil and natural gas, and is of minimal strategic importance to the West, so there seemed no reason to ponder future steps or devise new policy. The uprising there was an isolated event. Wish the Tunisians well and say goodbye.

We now know how incorrect this was. *Everyone,* presumably, was surprised by what transpired during the following weeks. But major powers are not supposed to be surprised. Although flawless prescience might not be expected, being able to respond coherently is.

Why countries around the world reacted so tentatively deserves analysis. Those wanting to place blame can begin with the intelligence agencies, diplomatic services, and others who are supposed to keep abreast of events on the ground. Like governments, major news organizations do not enjoy surprises, and their own information-gathering networks similarly failed to detect the fault lines from which such upheaval would emerge.

The principal villain was probably the lulling comfort of the status quo, which was so pleasing to those who held power in the region and their friends elsewhere. "Stability" had come to be so valued that even the Western democracies were willing to look the other way as that stability was sustained by police-state methods. The fact that tens of millions of Arabs hated the way things were going in their lives was either unnoticed or disregarded. Then in 2011, as mass demonstrations began in country after country, policymakers throughout the world scrambled to determine not just what was happening but how it affected their own national interests.

The major powers soon realized that a one-size-fits-all approach would not work. Aaron David Miller wrote that "the United States finds itself in terra incognita...without a unified doctrine to guide it. But the absence of such a lodestar is actually fortuitous. No single strategy could possibly accommodate the differences and variations in play or harmonize America's values, interests, and policies."[29]

Policymakers' work was complicated by the amount of information arriving and the speed with which it was delivered. Traditional patterns of information flow quickly proved obsolete. Intelligence agencies could not keep up with Twitter. Television networks were scooped by YouTube. Photojournalists were unable to match the content on Flickr. The sources for all this material were countless as individuals gathered and disseminated information on their own.

Within the resulting cacophony were valuable pieces of the puzzle that was the emerging Arab Spring. But the unprecedented task was to find those pieces and make sense of what was happening, state-by-state, and as a regional phenomenon. While policymakers tried to do this by first sorting out the events in Tunisia, revolution was going viral.

Egypt

There it was, for everyone to watch on Al Jazeera. The Tunisians were in the streets. They had had enough of a government that enriched insiders and left everyone else impoverished and without hope.

As Egyptians watched this, the similarities to their own situation were striking. Most Egyptians barely made enough money to survive. Jobs were nearly impossible to find. And yet the president's family and friends were amassing great wealth. Hosni Mubarak was just the Egyptian version of Zine el-Abidine Ben Ali. It was time for him to go. If Tunisia could have a revolution, why not Egypt as well?

Mubarak had held power for almost 30 years, and Egypt's riot police were adept at choking off demonstrations, using sheer numbers and escalating force to contain protests. In 2011, however, buoyed up by events in Tunisia, antigovernment activists employed sophisticated feints and other deception to evade security forces. Organizers publicly called for marches on January 25, the "Day of Rage," at 20 sites, but secretly organized another protest at a place only they knew about. Police showed up en masse at the 20 announced sites, but at the twenty-first site—a small plaza in front of a candy shop in Cairo's Bulaq al-Dakrour slum—no police were on hand. From there, marchers made their way to Tahrir Square. Because of their small number, the demonstrators soon were chased out of the square by police using tear gas and rubber bullets. But three days later, their ranks much larger, the protestors returned to Tahrir Square and stayed.[30] One protestor said of the police: "We saw them retreat in front of us as we marched to the square. It was an amazing feeling, them retreating, us marching forward. We won, they lost, and we both knew it."[31]

It is important to understand that the Egyptian protests were successful largely because they were not spontaneous; although organizers were inspired by Tunisians' courage, the Egyptian marches did not suddenly spring up as imitations of what had taken place in Tunisia. The principal organizers of the Egyptian effort had been working for at least three years, since the founding of the April 6 Youth Movement, which began as a Facebook group in 2008 supporting industrial workers and calling for a nation-wide strike on April 6 of that year. They also drew from established groups that were at odds with the government, such as *Kefaya* (Enough!) and labor organizations. Although they were not always visible, these activists met frequently to fine-tune their strategies and tactics.

The International Crisis Group reported that "one of the more striking features of the protest movement has been the absence of

leaders, a specific program, or a structure.... Rather than inspired
by a specific political agenda, it was fueled by a more abstract feeling
of fatigue and weariness vis-à-vis the state's predatory practices, corruption and arbitrariness, and the absence of any sense of collective
purpose.... At the head of the protestors' list was the demand that
Mubarak step down, 'in hours or days, not weeks or months.' "[32]

Successful revolutions are few and far between. Jack Goldstone
has noted that "for a revolution to succeed, a number of factors have
to come together. The government must appear so irremediably
unjust or inept that it is widely viewed as a threat to the country's
future; elites (especially in the military) must be alienated from the
state and no longer willing to defend it; a broad-based section of
the population, spanning ethnic and religious groups and socioeconomic classes, must mobilize; and international powers must either
refuse to step in to defend the government or constrain it from using
maximum force to defend itself. Revolutions rarely triumph because
these conditions rarely coincide."[33]

Mubarak, 82 years old at the time of the protests, seemed to not
comprehend the power of the storm swirling around him. He tried
to buy time, but the demonstrators' momentum increased. The
armed forces deserted him, refusing to use lethal force to break up
the protests and even protecting demonstrators from pro-Mubarak
gangs. The military moved into the vacuum created by Mubarak's
inability to lead, and took control of governing the country. This
has led some observers to debate whether Mubarak's fall was the
result of a popular revolt or was really a military coup.[34] Mubarak
resigned on February 11, little more than two weeks after the protests had begun.

Other governments within and outside the region were stunned
and alarmed. Mubarak may have been a corrupt despot, but he was
a known quantity, and in an unstable part of the world predictability
is highly valued. Across the spectrum, from Israel to Saudi Arabia
and from the United States to China, policymakers scrambled to
make sense of what was happening, determine how they would be
affected, and shape responses.

The United States had to scramble more than most because it had
embraced Mubarak so resolutely for so long. During the first days
of the protests in Egypt, White House foreign policy sages assumed
that Mubarak would survive. More important in terms of Arab

opinion, the White House was seen as *wanting* Mubarak to hold on. Democracy was not, after all, as important as a reliable ally.

On January 28, after several days of turmoil in Egypt, White House press secretary Robert Gibbs cautiously stated the US position in terms of aid given to the Mubarak government: "We will be reviewing our assistance posture based on events that take place in the coming days." A few hours later, President Obama said Egyptian authorities should "refrain from calling for any violence against peaceful protestors," and requested Mubarak to address his people's grievances, but he made no mention of the need for free elections.[35] Several days before that, as the Egyptian protests began, Secretary of State Clinton had said, "Our assessment is that the Egyptian government is stable and is looking for ways to respond to the legitimate needs and interests of the Egyptian people."[36]

The off-balance reaction of the Obama administration was strange partly because the president seemed to have recognized that trouble was looming in the region. In August 2010, he had sent a memo to his senior foreign policy team in which he acknowledged that "progress toward political reform and openness in the Middle East and North Africa lags behind other regions and has, in some cases, stalled." He cited "evidence of growing citizen discontent with the region's regimes," and noted that US allies in the region might "opt for repression rather than reform to manage domestic dissent." He added that "our regional and international credibility will be undermined if we are seen or perceived to be backing repressive regimes and ignoring the rights and aspirations of citizens." He asked for country-specific strategies related to political reform that the United States could endorse.[37]

And yet when Tunisia and then Egypt erupted, the United States moved slowly, apparently reluctant to abandon the comfortable status quo. One senior administration official said, "I don't think that because a group of young people get on the street that we are obliged to be for them."[38]

Obama himself, however, soon recognized the magnitude of what was happening and began to chart a course that would not only allow navigation through Egypt's stormy waters, but also reassure other Arab states—Saudi Arabia among them—that the United States had not decided to abandon its friends. An Obama adviser said: "Obama didn't give the Tahrir Square crowds every last thing they sought from him at the precise moment they sought it. But he went well beyond what many of America's allies in the region wished to see."[39]

The specter that Mubarak, the Saudis, and some others in the region cited was a surge of Islamist influence—"Egypt will be the new Iran." This tactic had been effective for years as a way to keep the United States from pushing old-line regimes toward meaningful reforms. The Muslim Brotherhood had long served Mubarak well in this regard, as he coolly used the West's Islamophobia to his advantage. But eventually, that charm no longer worked its magic.

All these political developments were being watched by much of the world. As will be detailed in the following chapter, the emotional ambiance within the region and far beyond was shaped by intensive live television coverage and a frantically busy online community. As far away as China, the inviolability of government power was newly questioned, if not (yet) assertively challenged.

Beyond Tunisia and Egypt

Because of the pervasive media coverage by major news organizations and citizen journalists, the reverberations from events in Tunisia and then Egypt were felt throughout the Arab world. The old-line rulers had been shaken not only by the activism in the streets, but also by what they saw as America's delayed but still abrupt dumping of Mubarak. They knew that the Egyptian had long been viewed by many US officials as an Arab good ol' boy, predictable and reliable. Aaron David Miller wrote, "When I worked at the State Department and would travel with secretaries James Baker, Warren Christopher, and Madeleine Albright, we always stopped in Cairo first to consult with Mubarak and, frankly, to enjoy his company. We looked at him as a friend."[40]

Several of the long-established monarchies in the region responded most adroitly: the Saudi royals poured money into the economy to at least superficially alleviate housing problems and food costs; King Abdullah of Jordan fired his prime minister, promised elections, and made visible efforts to connect with his people; in Morocco, King Mohammed VI made parliament appear more prominent while surrendering none of his own power. All of this may have been window-dressing, but it bought time for the monarchs during the period of greatest turmoil within the region.

The financial largesse was impressive even though the motivation behind it could be questioned.

- Algeria: $156 billion on new infrastructure projects; tax on sugar reduced;
- Bahrain: $100 million for families;
- Jordan: salary increases for the military and civil servants; tax cuts; aid for poor;
- Kuwait: $4,000 for each citizen; free food for 14 months; and
- Oman: 40 percent increase in the minimum wage; 50,000 new government jobs.[41]

Other Arab governments also made efforts that were clearly designed to buy loyalty, or at least peace. But the public was not always easily bought off. The situation of Bahrain and its autocratic ruling family illustrated the complexities of the region's politics that transcended financial concerns. The Sunni royal family rules a country estimated to be about 80 percent Muslim, of whom 70 percent are Shi'a. With petroleum refining, aluminum smelting, and a diversified economy, the country is prosperous, although many of its residents (many of whom are Shi'a) live in poverty. The US Fifth Fleet is based there, making the United States slow to criticize the regime. In February 2011, days after Mubarak had stepped down in Egypt, opponents of the Bahraini government took to the streets, demanding reforms. Unable to suppress this to his satisfaction, the king requested Saudi and Emirati forces to help restore order. One reason Saudi Arabia and the UAE were so willing to intervene was their belief that the Shi'a discontent was being orchestrated by Iran. Solid proof of that is hard to come by, although it is a plausible scenario and the intervention illustrated how on-edge some Sunni states are about Iranian meddling. This also affects the United States (and Israeli) positioning on reform efforts, as their support is most likely to be given to leadership that will checkmate Iran's ambitions.

Yemen offers another example of the difficulties the United States may have with its "friends." The government of President Ali Abdullah Saleh had proved fairly pliable in allowing the United States to use drones and other methods to hunt down Al Qaeda operatives within Yemen, but he proved intolerant of reformers and pushed his country toward bankruptcy and civil war. As of early

August 2011, Saleh remained in Saudi Arabia receiving medical care after being wounded during an attack on his residence in Sanaa at the beginning of June. His relatives and allies kept control while fighting against tribal leaders who wanted a new government. Saleh, who once likened governing Yemen to "dancing on the heads of snakes," showed no inclination to resign, although it was unclear if the Saudis would allow him to return to Yemen.[42] The United States made clear its distaste for Saleh's continuing regime, but not seeing a clear alternative and fearing that Al Qaeda in the Arabian Peninsula would have a safe haven in Yemen if Saleh were to leave, US policymakers did little to push him aside or to assist his opponents.

At least in the case of Libya there was no friendly relationship to consider. Muammar Qaddafi, a despot of questionable sanity, had ruled Libya since 1969. He had been tolerated for years because he rarely interfered in other country's affairs, particularly after he watched the United States invade Iraq and realized that Libya was probably also on the Bush administration's target list. And, of course, Libya produced a useful quantity of oil.

When a revolt against his rule began and Qaddafi threatened bloody reprisals against his opponents, the West summoned its collective indignation and, with the United States briefly in the vanguard, NATO began military operations, launching air strikes in support of rebel forces. Qaddafi, however, demonstrated considerable staying power, and the rebels demonstrated considerable ineptitude. But the tide shifted as the NATO strikes decimated Qaddafi's military infrastructure, and by September 2011, Qaddafi was on the run and the rebels' new government had taken over.

The most difficult decisions for outsiders were the ones taken about Syria. The initial demonstrations were small, and President Bashar Assad's government quickly labeled them as inconsequential trouble-making by the Muslim Brotherhood (that always-convenient villain), abetted by the sensationalist reporting of Al Jazeera. Many governments wanted to believe the truth of that. Syria had repeatedly been referred to as the keystone for any lasting agreement between Israel and the larger Arab community. Assad had compiled a mixed record: a willingness to talk reasonably with emissaries from the West and reckless ploys such as initiating a nuclear program and aiding Hezbollah. In any event, he and his father, Hafez, before him had ruled firmly for more than 40 years, and no feasible replacement was in sight. By summer 2011, the small demonstrations had grown in size and spread throughout much of the country, and they were increasingly met with vicious countermeasures by the government.

The rest of the world's anger grew and sanctions were imposed. On July 31, President Obama said: "I am appalled by the Syrian government's use of violence and brutality against its own people.... Once again, President Assad has shown that he is completely incapable and unwilling to respond to the legitimate grievances of the Syrian people. His use of torture, corruption and terror puts him on the wrong side of history and his people.... In the days ahead, the United States will continue to increase our pressure on the Syrian regime, and work with others around the world to isolate the Assad government and stand with the Syrian people."[43] By August 18, Obama had stepped up his rhetoric: "For the sake of the Syrian people, the time has come for President Assad to step aside."[44] Similar messages were delivered by Turkey and other countries that had previously been on relatively friendly terms with Assad.

The prospect of isolation and being told to step aside did not deter Assad. The wild card in the Syrian turmoil was once again Iran, more significantly than had been the case in Bahrain. To what extent would Iran help Assad, and to what extent would removal of Assad hurt Iran? Those questions were particularly important to Israel, which could tolerate Assad (again, the known-quantity factor) but would see any increased involvement by Iran as a serious threat. When Iran began issuing statements urging Assad to reduce the ferocity of his countermeasures against the insurgents, the puzzle became even more complicated.

This underscores the reality of the Arab Awakening as being much more than an insular upheaval. Outside players—Iran and NATO among them—became involved, and given the energy security issues that are inseparable from the politics of the region, most of the world's industrialized nations were paying close attention to events there even if they had difficulty formulating their responses.

★   ★   ★

Depending on the onlookers' outlook on political life, all this constituted either a colossal mess or a remarkably encouraging step toward democratization and better lives for millions in the Arab world. Unfortunately, much of the global public has come to expect real-time solutions to the crises they see reported in real time, and that is totally unrealistic. Substantive, institutional change takes time. Marwan Muasher, former foreign minister of Jordan, said of this: "One cannot expect this to be a linear process or to be done overnight. There were no real political parties, no civil society institutions ready to take over in any of these countries.... It is going to play out over the next 10 to 15 years before it settles down.... These people are experiencing democracy for the first time. They are going to make mistakes on the political and economic fronts. But I remain optimistic in the long run, because people have stopped feeling powerless."[45]

That could be said about many major political evolutions, such as the rebirth of Eastern Europe in the 1990s and even going back to the American War of Independence. One important difference between these earlier upheavals and those that began in Sidi Bouzid, Tunisia, in December 2010 is the presence of twenty-first-century media tools. They help drive events and set their pace. They shape expectations and put unprecedented pressure on policymakers. They impose transparency to a degree that foils those who hope that they might bloodily crush people's hopes without the rest of the world noticing.

This is the setting for real-time diplomacy in a media-centric world.

CHAPTER 2

THE MEDIA REVOLUTION

Media do not create revolutions; people with courage do.

Media can, however, accelerate the pace of a revolution and help build its constituency. When pitted against a government, a revolutionary movement can use media as an information equalizer in telling its story, managing logistics, and accomplishing the many small communications tasks that must happen in concert if the uprising is to succeed.

And within the world of twenty-first-century media, another revolution—this one based on the innovative intricacies of technology—is ongoing, as new devices and systems push aside the old. Think back to not too long ago when a few television channels and the dial telephone were the marvels of the time and were the principal "new" ways to get information in and out.

Communicating has always been essential during political turmoil. An organizer in Tunis posting news of a planned demonstration on Facebook may seem to have little in common with Paul Revere riding through Massachusetts in 1775 to warn that "the Redcoats are coming," but they shared the goal of alerting their colleagues to a crucial impending event. The Tunisian's message, however, could reach many thousands instantly, and within moments they could contact thousands of others. No horse needed.

The Middle East Media Environment

New media tools made their power felt suddenly and, for many, surprisingly. In July 2010, noted Arab journalist Rami Khouri wrote that the new media were "more like a stress reliever than a mechanism for political change." He added that blogging tended to make one a spectator rather than a participant, and stated: "We must face the fact that all the new media and hundreds of thousands of young bloggers from Morocco to Iran have not triggered a single significant or lasting change in Arab or Iranian political culture. Not a single one. Zero."[1]

Khouri may have been correct when he wrote that, but within six months the relationship between new media and political activism looked very different. What had changed? The media tools had improved somewhat and had become more widespread, but the crucial factor was political, not technological. The mix of despair and anger had reached the point at which it was shared by a significant portion of the public and could no longer be contained. Governments in Tunisia, Egypt, and elsewhere had not anticipated this—they did not expect an end to the docility they so assiduously enforced—and so they were unprepared to respond. Then the Bouazizi suicide (or de facto murder) happened, and the elements of the perfect political storm came together. They were aided—though by no means created—by media of various kinds.

US State Department official Alec Ross said that the Internet "acted as an accelerant" during the Arab Spring. Ross also observed that "networks disrupt the exercise of power. They devolve power from the nation state—from governments and large institutions—to individuals and small institutions. The overarching pattern is the redistribution of power from governments and large institutions to people and small institutions."[2] In a way, Ross was echoing Ronald Reagan, who in a 1989 speech said, "Technology will make it increasingly difficult for the state to control the information its people receive.... The Goliath of totalitarianism will be brought down by the David of the microchip."[3]

The ascendance of new, Internet-based media was a continuation of change within the Arab media world that had begun with the birth of Al Jazeera in 1996 and continued with the growing influence of pan-Arab media. Mohammed El Oifi wrote that Al Jazeera's "Arab nationalism has in some ways become the basis of a sharp critique of Arab rulers who have come to favor the fragmentation of the Arab public sphere, sacrificing thereby the ideal of Arab unity."[4] Al Jazeera pits its influence and commitment to pan-Arabism against the "every country for itself" approach that has become common in the Arab world.

Individual Arab journalists' attitudes reflect the appeal of pan-Arabism. Lawrence Pintak reported that based on a survey he and colleagues conducted in 2006, "fully one-third identify first with the Arab region; the Muslim world comes a close second. Only 15 percent identified first with their country of citizenship. These figures show the degree to which Arab journalists are at the forefront of an emerging pan-Arab identity—call them border guards of a new Arab consciousness—focused on reshaping the region for a more politically inclusive future."[5]

Although Al Jazeera has become one of the world's best known brands, its notoriety should not be allowed to overshadow other developments in Arab broadcasting. Its principal competitor is Al Arabiya, created in 2003 and funded by Saudi investors. It has positioned itself as a quieter, more conservative, more balanced alternative to the Qatar-based channel. Al Arabiya does not shy away from rigorous reporting; its coverage of Arab terrorist groups has been particularly courageous. The channel also does not back away from criticizing Al Jazeera. Nabil Khatib, Al Arabiya's executive editor, said in 2011, "Journalism is not about supporting the revolution. It's not about trying to act as a political party who's trying to be activist rather than to offer information." Al Jazeera, he added, was "trying to be part of the conflict."[6]

Al Jazeera and Al Arabiya are the brightest stars in the expanding constellation of Arab satellite television, which includes more than 500 channels, most of which provide entertainment or religious programming rather than news. Less noticed has been the gradual development of privately owned national channels that appeal to viewers who want news more tightly focused than what the regional broadcasters offer but who do not trust the traditional government-run media outlets. In Egypt, private broadcasters ON-TV and Dream-TV were prohibited by the Mubarak government from airing regular newscasts, but were allowed to produce news discussion programs. So, during the Egyptian uprising, while Al Jazeera, Al Arabiya, and other regional and international channels provided live reporting from the streets, ON-TV and Dream offered interviews with key participants in the revolution. As political conversation in Egypt becomes more open and more intense, these local channels will be able to offer much more Egypt-based coverage than the regional channels will provide and are likely to establish a solid audience base.[7]

With the fall of Mubarak, 16 low-budget television channels quickly opened, one of which is Cairo-based January 25 TV. This channel offers shows such as *Hashtag*, which collects news from Facebook, Twitter, and YouTube to broadcast to the large audience that has television but not Internet at home. These channels reflect the new spirit of intellectual independence among journalists. One of 25 TV's reporters said of their programming, "We're broadcasting what Egyptians need to hear, not what the state wants us to say."[8]

Television has been around for a long time without doing much by itself to facilitate revolutions. The difference today is the existence of an array of new media tools that have fostered a "television-plus" environment that supports the growth of political activism.

The most pervasive communication tool—even more common than television—is the mobile phone. Statistics follow in the next section of this chapter, but for now consider the sociopolitical effect of this nearly ubiquitous device. There is, of course, the basic telephone call—the unprecedented intense connectivity among family members, friends, and like-minded activists that used to be possible only from a fixed position but now is feasible from almost anywhere. In wealthy countries, smartphones with Internet connection are plentiful, but in most of the Middle East, mobile phone use had been limited, until recently, to voice and text messages. Throughout the world, the smartphone is gaining market share. In 2009, 172 million smartphones were sold; in 2011, 468 million; and projected for 2015, 631 million.[9] This are small numbers compared to the more than five billion cell phones in use worldwide, but this kind of growth means that many more people will soon be able to access a richer array of content through their phones.

The most useful accessory during the Arab Spring was the camera that so many phones feature. Powerful still and moving images undermined government versions of events in Bahrain, Syria, and other places. When officials tried to mask their violence with bland lies, citizens provided the images that revealed the truth. Through these images, events became stories that were ingrained with emotional and political power.[10]

★   ★   ★

Another basic tool used during the events of 2011 was the blog. Bloggers had been at work since the 1990s, but they gained greater notice during the 2003 invasion of Iraq.[11] Salam Pax, an Iraqi living in Baghdad, provided descriptions of life in the war zone, as did members of the US military. Howard Kurtz described the blogs about

Iraq as "idiosyncratic, passionate, and often profane, with the sort of intimacy and attitude that are all but impossible in newspapers and on television."[12] These early blogs were part of a new "citizen journalism," which has contributed to greatly expanding the information universe and to changing the conventions of news delivery. Some aspects of this more freewheeling approach are good; the intensity of personal experience elevates the emotional power of quasi-journalistic storytelling. On the other hand, blogs and other populist news forms sometimes do not adhere to the principles of journalism that place a premium on accuracy and balance, and readers may be susceptible to being duped by blogs that are more fiction than fact.

In their early days, one difficulty with blogs was finding them amidst the vast amount of online content, but today aggregators such as *Huffington Post* and Global Voices feature noteworthy blog content. Rebecca MacKinnon, cofounder of Global Voices, said, "Our job is to curate the conversation that is happening all over the Internet with people who really understand what is going on."[13] This is a new facet of journalism—not so much that individuals are offering their take on events, but that their versions are so easily accessible. The individual blogger, writing about events on the streets of Damascus or Manama, may well be read by many thousands throughout the world, and the report may be amplified by major news organizations picking it up or pursuing the information on their own.

The newer incarnations of social media, such as Twitter and Facebook, are further examples of the marriage of personal political communication and journalism. To a considerable extent, these media are used more for reporting than for proselytizing (albeit with some mixing of the two). When one opens the Twitter site, the question posed is, "What's happening?" This replaced "What are you doing?" which lent itself to recitations of personal trivia. The new query is likely to elicit a more reportorial response, although plenty of nonsense still pops up. Although Tweets themselves are limited to 140 characters and so are basically a headline service, they can provide links to more substantive content, including video. In the midst of a street demonstration, the terseness that the 140-character limit requires works just fine.

Facebook offers a mix of journalism, declamation, and notice board. The "friend"-to-"friend" multiplier effect can build audience at great speed. The best-known Facebook page during the Egyptian uprising was "We Are All Khaled Said," named after a young man who was beaten to death by Egyptian police in Alexandria. This page not only drew worldwide attention to the brutal murder of Said, but also came to symbolize the refusal of many Egyptians to continue to turn away when government brutality took place. It publicized events taking place in Egypt's streets and underscored the commitment of many Egyptians to finally bringing about substantive change in their personal and political lives. This was one of the foundation stones of the revolution, an electronic gathering place for people who were frustrated, angry, and determined to succeed. As of mid-2011, the Arabic page of "We Are All Khaled Said" had 1.5 million "friends," while the English-language page had 135,000.[14] In a global context, with more than 800 million users and still rapidly growing, Facebook, if it were a physical nation, would be the third-most populous state in the world, behind only China and India.

Although new media attracted most of the attention during the Arab Awakening, newspapers showed that they should not be discounted. Before the demonstrators of 2011 began Tweeting or posting on Facebook walls, independent newspapers, such as *Al-Masry Al-Youm* in Egypt, had laid the groundwork for change through their brave coverage of government corruption and brutality. *Al-Masry Al-Youm* has a website, an iPad app, and an online English-language edition, but its basic Arabic print version remains heavily depended on a public that is not willing or, in many cases, not able to wholly switch to electronic news providers.[15]

In Egypt, daily newspaper circulation is more than 4.3 million, the highest in the Arab world. (Globally, newspaper circulation rose by 6 percent between 2005 and 2009, led by countries such as India, where 110 million papers are sold each day.) Newspaper content reflects the rise of other news media, as can be seen in newspapers providing elaborate graphics and increasing the argumentative flair of their news coverage. This harkens back to the eighteenth century's coffee houses where pamphlets and broadsides, the forerunners of newspapers, were discussed loudly and helped shape popular political debate. The *Economist* recently stated that "the Internet is making news more participatory, social, diverse, and partisan, reviving the discursive ethos of the era before mass media. That will have profound effects on society and politics."[16]

New media offerings have had to contend with the state-run Arab news organization that for so many years dominated the media landscape and devoted themselves to legitimizing the regimes that they, in one way or another, served. Their work was made easier by the failure of news media elsewhere in the world to persistently and thoroughly cover human rights abuses and the protests that occurred periodically and usually briefly. One of the reasons so many people throughout the world were astounded by the Arab Awakening was that the news media on which they relied had largely ignored the deteriorating social conditions and growing restiveness in many Arab states, and so the uprisings seemed to come out of nowhere. Blogs became tools that people in Tunisia, Egypt, and elsewhere in the region could use to fill in the contextual gaps left by mainstream news coverage, but few among the ranks of policymakers or the general public seemed to pay them much attention.[17]

To better understand these effects, it is useful to consider some statistics that show how different forms of media are becoming more pervasive in the Arab world and elsewhere.

Shifting Media Preferences

Among traditional media, the shift from terrestrial to satellite television has grown more pronounced. As of December 2010, 138 terrestrial channels operated in the Arab world, most of which were government-owned. The number of these channels has been holding constant, and only in Palestine and Iraq are the majority of channels privately owned. Meanwhile, the number of free-to-air satellite channels has continued to grow, increasing by more than 10 percent between April 2010 and April 2011. As of mid-2011, 538 channels were being broadcast on the region's three principal satellites: Arabsat, Nilesat, and Noorsat. More than two-thirds of these satellite channels are privately owned.[18]

Newer media have made varying degrees of progress in reaching larger numbers of Arab users. A Gallup survey found that between 2009 and 2010, cellular phone access among young Arabs (aged 15–29), rose from 79 percent to 87 percent. In high-income Arab countries, more than 98 percent of young Arabs used cell phones, and even in the low-income countries the figure was 81 percent.[19] Most of these cell phones are simple handsets, not smartphones, and

can be used for voice conversations and text messages, but not for
accessing the Internet.

Internet use remains much less widespread, although it keeps
growing. Among young Arabs, access at home during this period
grew from 19 to 22 percent, while access in the community rose
from 59 to 62 percent. This difference underscores the importance,
particularly in developing nations, of Internet cafes, schools, and
other public spots where the necessary technology is available to
those who might not be able to personally afford to acquire it. This
access is important not only for gathering news, but also for searching for job opportunities and otherwise connecting with the economic and social life of the community.[20]

Internet penetration in the Middle East varies substantially from
country to country. As of mid-2011, according to *Internet World
Stats*, penetration in Iraq, Libya, and Yemen was less than 10 percent,
while in Qatar and the United Arab Emirates the figure had climbed
above 65 percent. In percentage terms, the growth rate of Internet
use since 2000 has been huge in some nations; even Yemen has
seen user growth rise by 15,560 percent during the decade. As of
June 2011, Internet penetration in Tunisia was 34 percent, while in
Egypt it was 25 percent. In Syria, it was 20 percent, and in Libya
5 percent.[21] Despite the encouraging rate of expansion in some
countries, Internet connectivity in the region has a long way to go
before it matches television or mobile phone penetration.

For those in the Arab states who have Internet access, Facebook
has become a popular tool, especially after it introduced an Arabic-
language interface in early 2009. Despite the Arabic accessibility,
almost all the users in Tunisia, Morocco, and Algeria still use the
French version, and many elsewhere in the region use English.

This says something about the Facebook community's socioeconomic status, and it should be taken into account when evaluating the role of social media in the Arab world and in developing
countries elsewhere. Social media users do not necessarily reflect the
larger population, which includes millions of poor, rural, illiterate,
or semiliterate people who have little in common with young, well-
educated activists. Granted, these activists may be driving events at a
given moment, but policymakers would be wise not to read Tweets
or Facebook announcements as representative of broad public sentiment. When reports are issued about what Tweeters or Facebook

users are thinking and doing, it should be remembered that this does not necessarily reflect the disposition of the larger populace.

Nevertheless, according to the Dubai School of Government's periodic *Arab Social Media Report,* the growth in Arab use of Facebook has been noteworthy:

- The total number of Facebook users in the Arab world stood at 27,711,503 as of April 2011, up from 21,377,282 in January 2011, an increase of 30 percent. The number had almost doubled since the same time the previous year (14,791,972 in April 2010).
- At the beginning of April 2011, the country average for Facebook user penetration in the Arab region was just over 7.5 percent, up from just under 6 percent at the end of 2010.[22]

As for Twitter, the numbers of users are lower. In its study of social media use, the Dubai School of Government estimated that in early 2011 there were about 6.6 million Arab Twitter users, with slightly more than a million of them using Twitter actively. The study also found the following:

- During the first quarter of 2011, these "active users" generated 22,750,000 Tweets. The estimated number of daily Tweets was 252,000 per day—175 Tweets a minute or roughly 3 Tweets a second.
- The estimated number of daily Tweets per active user in the Arab region in the first quarter of 2011 was 0.81.
- The most popular trending hashtags across the Arab region in the first quarter of 2011 were #egypt (with 1.4 million mentions in the Tweets generated during this period) #jan25 (1.2. million mentions), #libya (990,000 mentions), and #bahrain (640,000 mentions).[23]

(As a comparison to the three Tweets-per-second average cited here, the worldwide record in this category, as of summer 2011, was 7,196 Tweets per second during the final moments of the Women's World Cup in which Japan defeated the United States.[24])

The surge in social media use, particularly among young Arabs, is part of the larger context of the Arab Awakening, but it should be remembered that many of the people out on the streets of Tunis, Cairo, Sanaa, Manama, and elsewhere live outside the world of the

Internet and its communication tools. The people most victimized by the economic inequities of the Arab regimes were the poorest, and many of them poured out of the slums because of what they saw on a "community TV" in a neighborhood coffee shop or what they heard by word of mouth from friends and family about the political earthquake that was shaking their country. They weren't looking at laptop or smartphone screens; they didn't need them to be ready and finally willing to act to change their lives.

Those who did have access to social media found that they were valuable tools in mobilizing and organizing, and were useful in helping those on the streets outmaneuver and outwit their flailing governments.

Putting Media to Work

As the uprisings began to take hold, organizers used media in various ways, ranging from communicating within a neighborhood to reaching the outside world. The audiences were a mix of local, national, regional, and global activists and spectators, many of them eager to learn from their colleagues' successes and failures.

Egypt

Online communication had been used by Egyptian antigovernment organizers for years before the Arab Spring, particularly by the April 6 Youth Movement, which by early 2009 reportedly had 70,000 members. Among its projects was compilation of an online manual for protestors, which covered topics ranging from security measures to the usefulness of graffiti.[25] Videos placed on YouTube, and then further disseminated through blogs, helped maintain an undercurrent of outrage during the years leading up to the 2011 uprising. Wael Abbas, one of the best-known bloggers, posted a cell phone video of Cairo police officers torturing a man. Egyptians and the rest of the world could see how the police state operated, and once this door was opened other videos of similar incidents emerged. With the world watching, the government had to act, and when the police officers were prosecuted, bloggers kept the public up to date on the court proceedings.[26] This online alternative to state-run news media developed an avid audience that was large and loud enough to put the government on notice that its abusive behavior would not be ignored.

When the street demonstrations began, organizers used their own cell phone cameras to record arrests and excessive force used by police. Their Facebook pages contained useful advice for protestors: don't disrupt traffic; display only Egyptian flags, not partisan emblems; bring plenty of water; and so on.[27] Tunisian demonstrators who had gotten a head start on the Arab uprisings offered their own suggestions on Facebook, such as, "Advice to the youth of Egypt: put vinegar or onion under your scarf for tear gas."[28]

While on the streets, demonstrators found Twitter particularly useful both to report what was going on, which was often valuable in boosting morale, and to update locations of the protest marches.[29] One activist wrote that Twitter "is easy and flexible to do from your mobile. If we have a lot of action here I might do as many as 20 or 30 Tweets a day."[30] As the action on the streets increased, the Egyptian government was mounting a media counterattack. According to the International Crisis Group, "State television had initially tried to minimize or ignore the protests—by emphasizing the government's concessions and focusing on the violence and looting—but when foreign governments began to condemn the regime for its conduct, the regime sought to turn the situation to its advantage. It portrayed the protests as products of dangerous foreign meddling and the protestors as agents of radical Islam, Israel, or the West."[31] The state channels also covered pro-Mubarak demonstrations heavily, and famously showed images of a quiet bridge across the Nile while nearby hundreds of thousands of demonstrators were staging their protest. One antigovernment activist, composer Ammar El Sherei—who was finally allowed on government-run Channel One—asked, "Why is Egyptian TV not a source of information? Why did you force us to turn to Al Jazeera, Al Arabiya, and CNN?"[32]

When regime officials realized how widely mobile phones were being used, they ordered Egypt's principal mobile phone service, Vodaphone, to send government-written messages to its customers. Some gave locations of progovernment rallies, and others tried to turn the tide of public opinion: one urged "Youth of Egypt, beware of rumors and listen to the sound of reason," and another called on "Egypt's honest and loyal men to confront the traitors and criminals."[33]

More significantly, on January 28, 2011, the Egyptian government severed the country from the global Internet. Egypt, like many countries, connects to the Internet through a small number of portals to the outside world, which the government controls. State-owned Telecom Egypt, which owns almost all the fiber-optic cables of the country, made the shutdown easier for the government. Because so many of Egypt's internal networks rely on systems outside the country—such as the e-mail servers run by Google, Microsoft, and Yahoo—the country's domestic Internet was also crippled by the cutoff.[34]

The blackout was lifted after five days. Not only the protestors were cut off, but so too were international businesses operating within Egypt. The affected businesspeople presumably screamed loudly, which may be the reason the closure was made so brief. But by the time the government made its move, the uprising had so much momentum that the shutdown was of minimal consequence, but it was a reminder that in authoritarian countries the freedom of connectivity provided by the Internet can swiftly be taken away.

Part of the uprising's momentum was to be seen in the content of traditional media venues—those not tied to the Internet. Organizers sent times and places of forthcoming protests to Al Jazeera, and the channel promptly announced them to its huge audience (which was one reason the Mubarak government also knocked Al Jazeera off the air). Meanwhile, on call-in radio programs, the public was finding its voice. After hearing a caller denounce Mubarak on the air, one activist said: "Listen to that. The revolution is already here."[35]

Syria

For a while in 2011, Syria seemed impervious to the events transpiring in nearby Arab countries. Bashar al-Assad's grip on power appeared to be firm; his security apparatus was tough and efficient, and he enjoyed personal popularity, especially among a relatively small, but influential, segment of the population.

But then there was Al Jazeera, on which Syrians watched other Arabs demand change, and there were social media—not widely used, but available enough to be helpful to dissidents who wanted reform. As Hosni Mubarak was about to be toppled, the Assad government announced it was lifting its ban on Facebook. This was more a gesture than a meaningful change, as plenty of Syrians had been using international proxy servers to access Facebook and other sites. The popularity of these media continued to grow; the Facebook page "The Syrian Revolution 2011" had more than 250,000 friends by mid-summer 2011.

When Syria's demonstrations began, protestors' numbers were just in the few thousands. As their efforts began, they lit fires on rooftops to see how many others would show support by doing the same. The government contributed to its own problems by over-reacting. On February 16, a scuffle between a vendor and a police officer in Damascus brought out a crowd chanting, "The Syrian people will not be humiliated." In Deraa two weeks later, security forces arrested a group of teenagers and younger children, charging them with painting antigovernment graffiti on walls. When released a month later, some of the children showed visible signs of torture. While this was going on, the government was blaming "Islamists" and foreign agents for causing the trouble, and President Assad cited a need to purge "saboteurs" from the country.[36]

Among the Syrian public, unhappiness became anger, and from outside the country Syrian expatriates became involved. Some called into Syria to collect information and then Tweeted it. Others sent satellite phones and phone cards to help activists avoid surveillance. And all the while, Al Jazeera and other regional and international news organizations were providing Syrians and others images that showed government tanks blasting into cities such as Hama and bloody victims of the government crackdown lying in the streets. Protestors used their cell phone cameras to record these events and then used social media programs such as Qik to send them out of the country where friends could upload them onto YouTube. Then the Arab and international television channels picked up the videos, and Syrians and the rest of the world could see what was happening. By mid-June 2011, activists had uploaded more than 250 videos to the YouTube channel, Freedom4566, and they had been viewed more than 220,000 times.

Another Syrian media project is Shaam News Network, which defines itself this way: "Shaam News Network, SNN, is a group of patriotic Syrian youth activists demanding the freedom and dig-nity for the Syrian people and supporting the Syrian peoples' efforts for a democratic and peaceful change in Syria. SNN does not have any affiliation with any Syrian opposition parties or other states."[37] Shaam has content on Twitter, Facebook, and YouTube, and it serves as a resource for news organizations elsewhere that have faced dif-ficulties in covering events in Syria. It is the kind of operation that does not cost much to set up and its simple format is perfect for tech-savvy activists trying to outwit a government.

One young Damascus-based activist told a reporter how she and her colleagues went about their work: "We use a proxy server and change it almost every day. Today most young Syrians have mobile phones with high-quality cameras, so each one has become like a journalist. I upload videos and statements from Internet cafes. I leave after 10 minutes and don't come back to the same one for a long time."[38]

Protest organizers knew that the Syrian government was trying to track them by scanning Facebook and Twitter and looking for hints about identities and protest locations. Also, pro-Assad Syrians have their own Facebook pages. As of August 2011, the "Bashar al-Asad" page had more than 197,000 friends.[39] Progovernment spokespersons also alleged, sometimes correctly, that some of the antiregime videos were phony, showing footage that supposedly depicted Syrian unrest but actually consisted of images from earlier, unrelated incidents in Iraq and Lebanon.[40]

As this is written, Syria remains in bloody turmoil, with the international community pushing President Assad to commit to substantive reforms or step aside. Syria had been a tightly controlled country, and news of events there during the Arab Awakening was far less accessible by the international public than was information about the uprisings in Tunisia, Egypt, Yemen, and elsewhere. But still the information got out, seriously damaging Assad's claims to legitimacy and illustrating how information will find a way, through one medium or another, to reach domestic and international publics.

The Syrian case reflects the partial decline of state-imposed secrecy. Twenty years before, the Syrian government (then led by Bashar Assad's father) could probably have imposed a near-total news blackout, while it dealt however bloodily with protests. Just as WikiLeaks showed that "secret" documents can find their way to the public, so too have citizen media proved that when a state acts reprehensibly, the world will learn of it.

By late summer 2011, Syrian demonstrators were chanting, "We will not kneel," and the Assad government was realizing that it could not make them do so.

Elsewhere in the Region

Events in Tunisia and Egypt moved at speeds so fast as to be difficult to believe. Two of the region's most entrenched leaders were dethroned within a few weeks. Elsewhere, however, matters were more complicated, as the Syrian case illustrates. In Libya, a civil war began. In Bahrain, repression maintained much of the status quo ante. In Saudi Arabia, the monarchy seemed to have a firm hold on power, but social media use was spreading and gradually chipping away at the geriatric leadership's control over Saudi society. In Palestine, the region's revolutions seemed to have little effect. In Yemen, Jordan, and other states, stalemate took hold, at least for the time being. And in nearby Iran, some lessons about the limitations on social media's role were becoming clear. This is not the place for detailed recitations or analysis of the political events that occurred in these places, but there are media-related developments worth noting.

Like almost everything else in Libya, the country's telecommunications infrastructure was controlled by Muammar Qaddafi, with the entire system, including the Libyana cell phone service, which was based in Tripoli and designed for surveillance by Qaddafi's intelligence service. When anti-Qaddafi rebels began their uprising in Eastern Libya, cell phone service in that part of the country was cut off, and rebel soldiers on the battlefield needed to use signal flags to communicate with one another. One of the rebel commanders said of this, "Qaddafi forced us back to the stone age." In response, some Libyan expatriates designed a way to hijack the Libyana signal and set up a separate network. Doing so was not easy. Huawei Technologies Ltd., which was one of the contractors that had set up Libyana, refused to sell equipment for the rebels' venture. But the United Arab Emirates quietly came to the rescue, using its Etisalat telecommunications company to acquire the needed equipment, and Free Libyana began operating in the rebel-held eastern parts of the country.[41]

After Tripoli was seized by the rebels, the extent of the Qaddafi regime's electronic surveillance became clear. All international telephone calls going in and out of the country had been logged and monitored through a system provided by a South African company. A unit of a French company had provided the Libyans with a system that allowed observing network traffic and reading e-mails.[42]

In Bahrain, the uprising was cut short by the forceful intervention of the country's security forces, aided by Saudi and UAE reinforcements. As in many places in the Arab world, bloggers were writing about politics, but their numbers were small—one study estimated that only 150 were online in Bahrain in 2010. Of these, only 40 qualified as "political," and almost all were written in English. The country's sectarian divide between Shia and Sunni was reflected in blogs in early 2011. These noted that some Sunni Bahrainis who were unhappy with the government stayed away from protests because they perceived them to be more pro-Shia than anti-regime. Similarly on Facebook, competing sites sought to develop their own constituencies.[43]

Although there were some efforts to build unity, such as a "Not Shii, Not Sunni, Just Bahraini" online project, the Bahrain experience illustrates the limitations of media-based organizing. Politics, especially politics with religious hues, can trump connectivity.

To the relief of the Saudi royal family, the Arab Spring created just a passing breeze in the kingdom, at least for the moment. The Saudi rulers have long tried to insulate their country against the politics and culture of the rest of the world. The Internet is available, but its use is rigorously controlled by measures such as having cameras in Internet cafes and preventing access to sites deemed to contain "content in violation of Islamic tradition or national regulations."[44] Online connections to the global Internet are available through just two nodes, and Internet providers must connect through them. Bloggers and proprietors of all websites, chat rooms and the like have been ordered to register and get a license issued by the Ministry of Culture and Information, or else face a fine of up to 100,000 Saudi riyals (about US$26,000).[45]

When severe floods hit Jeddah in late 2009, Saudis used Twitter to criticize the government's response. In June 2011, when Manal al-Sharif, a Saudi woman, was jailed for nine days for driving a car, more than 30,000 comments—most supporting her—appeared on Twitter within the next few days. On the other side of the ideological spectrum, conservatives created a YouTube channel, CH905, to showcase the conservative messages of prominent Wahhabi traditionalist clerics.

Despite controls imposed by the government, Saudis are steadily increasing their use of these media. Neil MacFarquhar wrote that social media seem "tailor-made for Saudi Arabia, where public gatherings are illegal, women are strictly forbidden to mix with unrelated men, and people seldom mingle outside their family." He added that social liberals and religious conservatives now compete for online followers, and so have become more flexible in some of their issues positions.[46]

Palestinian activists have found mixed success in their online efforts. In March 2011, the "People Want to End the Division" Facebook page called for rallies to urge Hamas and Fatah to stop feuding. Close to 41,000 people said they would attend the rallies, and another 6,700 said they would try to be there. When the rallies took place, only 4,000 showed up in Ramallah, 1,500 in Nablus, and 3,000 in the Gaza Strip. Once again, political complexities and uncertainties outmatched the organizational strengths of online media. Palestinians have also faced difficulties with providers. A Facebook page calling for a Third Intifada was taken down by Facebook after the Israeli government complained that it was inciting violence.[47]

Going outside the Arab states to Iran, where the postelection uprising of 2009 had briefly raised hopes, skepticism has tempered expectations about what media can accomplish in the face of a government that will do anything necessary to retain power.

Golnaz Esfandiari, an Iranian and a senior correspondent with Radio Free Europe/Radio Liberty, has pointed out that much of the purported clout of Twitter during events in Iran is myth. Three of the most prominent Twitter accounts that carried reports about the situation in Tehran and even urged people to "take to the streets" were written by contributors in the United States, Turkey, and Switzerland. She noted that many of the Tweets cited by the Western press were in English, and that "no one seemed to wonder why people trying to coordinate protests in Iran would be writing in any language other than Farsi." She further wrote that "good old-fashioned word of mouth was by far the most influential medium used to shape the postelection opposition activity. . . . Twitter was definitely not a major communications tool for activists on the ground in Iran."[48]

Esfandiari's article is a useful corrective to the case presented by those who put far too much faith in social media, to the exclusion of much else, when citing the most useful tools in the mobilization of efforts to bring about political change. Twitter and other media mechanisms can, however, be extremely valuable in other ways. Esfandiari wrote: "Twitter played an important role in getting word about events in Iran out to the wider world. Together with YouTube, it helped focus the world's attention on the Iranian people's fight for democracy and human rights. New media over the last year created and sustained unprecedented international moral solidarity with the Iranian struggle—a struggle that was being bravely waged many years before Twitter was ever conceived."[49]

This connection to the larger world is valuable in itself, and the use of this bridge by Iranian dissidents enraged the government there. As the "global village" has become less a theory and more a reality, what other residents of the village think of events matters more, particularly to countries that aspire to regional or worldwide leadership roles. New media can do much to advance or undermine those aspirations.

★   ★   ★

Whether blogs, Tweets, Facebook or YouTube postings, or other social media tools are being employed, the effects of creating content on the individuals who do so tend to be overlooked. This does not refer to the work of professional geeks who live online or the politically courageous who have spoken out and frequently been penalized—sometimes harshly—for doing so. Instead, this is about the empowerment of previously disengaged citizens who discover that they now have a far-reaching and relatively safe means of expressing themselves. From the brief Tweet to the lengthy blog, people can shove aside the frustration of keeping silent in the face of political forces they disdain. The writing as well as the reading matters. Literary snobs and political experts might look down at the sometimes convoluted language and naive political views they see in these venues, but this is the discourse of democracy. It is part of what the Arab Awakening is about, and if the spirit of 2011 spreads—as it assuredly will—so will this newly liberated political speech. It will change the world.

For those who want to learn from and perhaps emulate the Arab Awakening, no foolproof formulae emerge from the cases cited above—just suggestions about ways that political action might benefit from diverse forms of communication technology. Although some tools will work better than others in particular situations—and choosing which can be a crucial decision for activists and governments—these technologies have at least one thing in common: the speed with which they can affect events and, therefore, the speed at which interested parties must react.

If policymakers are to effectively manage information moving at such a fast pace, they must understand the varied elements of real-time media and incorporate the new information flow into a carefully designed decision-making process.

Media Effects on Policy Responses

Information is out there—lots of it—and it is easily accessible, if you know where to look. In one form or another it is published through social media or more traditional venues and is available to the public. This is open-source intelligence, which is where agencies such as the CIA find 90 percent of the information they need. But it does not just fall into your hands. Some searching is required, and policymakers must be committed and organized enough to mine the online world for this material.

This did not happen, at least not thoroughly enough, during the first months of 2011. Many governments appeared baffled by events in the Arab world and responded sluggishly. US senator Dianne Feinstein said, "I don't believe there was any intelligence on what was happening on Facebook or Twitter or the organizational effort to put these protests together."

Feinstein did not label this an intelligence "failure," saying, "I would call it a big intelligence wakeup. . . . Open-source material has to become much more significant in the analysis of intelligence."[50]

Issues of quantity make this analysis difficult. During the cold war, the process involved reading newspapers, magazines, scholarly journals, and the like, and monitoring some radio broadcasts—an often tedious process, but manageable in terms of reviewing a finite number of sources. Today, all those traditional sources remain (although almost all can be found online), but they are joined by countless electronic dispatches from governments, organizations, and individuals. Some of these contain useful bits of information, but many more are worthless. (The worst are those that seem interesting but turn out to be fabrications.) Computer programs can search the Web and mobile phone traffic for keywords, and this electronic digging sometimes turns up gems, but computerized scrutiny is less than ideal for spotting nuance and trends.

Even when apparently good material is gathered, what do you do with it once you have it? How much consequence (and veracity) should be ascribed to a Tweet from Damascus or a YouTube video from Tripoli? Further, what happens if a government shuts down the Internet, as the Mubarak regime did, and suddenly this valued channel of information is choked off? How much effort should be devoted to developing technological bypasses for such cases? Are old-fashioned human intelligence assets available to fill the gap until the cyber world can again be accessed?

These procedural issues require policy decisions, just as do the substantive matters addressed in the communications themselves. As an adjunct to the concept of "Internet freedom" articulated by Secretary Clinton and others, the means of maintaining that freedom must be created. This is a matter of principle as well as practicality. As dependence on information supplied by new media grows, the flow of that information will need protection.

And yet, this is complicated on several levels. In 2009, the US State Department licensed "Haystack," a tool to help Iranians elude their government's Internet censors while remaining anonymous. But when Haystack went live in 2010, an independent team cracked its code in six hours and proved that the Iranian government could determine users' locations and identities. Two other tools, "Freegate" and "Ultrasurf," were developed by the US-based Global Internet Freedom Consortium (GIFC), which is run by the Falun Gong. When the US government funded these circumvention tools, which worked properly, the Chinese government protested strongly, raising the question of whether supporting the GIFC was worth damaging US-China relations.[51]

In its 2011 report on Internet freedom, the Center for a New American Security recommended that the United States bankroll the development of new technologies that would aid dissidents around the world. The report stated: "The U.S. government should continue to fund technologies other than firewall-evasion tools, including those that help dissidents maintain digital security, ensure mobile access, and reconstitute websites after a cyber attack."[52]

When they are developing guidelines related to protecting media use, policymakers should also factor in the potential for harm that media possess. Sometimes media can have the effect of exerting deadly force. This is nothing new; cases to come before international tribunals have included those of Julius Streicher, publisher of the anti-Semitic Nazi newspaper *Der Sturmer,* who was sentenced to death at Nuremberg in 1946, and radio broadcasters from Rwanda, who urged Hutus to murder Tutsis during the 1994 genocide and were sentenced to lengthy prison sentences by the International Criminal Tribunal.

Episodes of criminal media use that occurred occasionally in the past have become more persistent today, particularly some terrorist organizations' sophisticated adaptation of media assets to advance their cause. Al Qaeda has its own production company, As Sahab, that creates videos for online viewing. Anwar al-Awlaki, who was head of Al Qaeda in the Arabian Peninsula before being killed in a US drone attack,, had been called by some "the Bin Laden of the Internet" and had adherents including three of the 9/11 hijackers, the perpetrators of the failed 2009 Christmas Day airliner bombing and the 2009 shootings at Fort Hood, and others. Awlaki, who was born in the United States and held US and Yemeni citizenship, disseminated his sermons, in Arabic and English, through numerous websites. US counterterrorism officials had been particularly worried about him because his English-language Internet videos were designed to recruit American Muslims to stage attacks within the United States.

For terrorists, new media are, collectively, a transformative mechanism that offers endless possibilities for communication and expansion. The real power of terrorism lies not in the acts of individuals, however horrific they may be, but rather in the activities of terrorists in networks that allow secure coordination within even loosely knit terrorist organizations. New media are crucial in helping terrorist groups to endure—to sustain themselves by reaching various publics and to create a virtual impermeability that protects their operations. These media allow terrorist groups to become regional and even global players, sometimes punching above their weight in propaganda terms and building support from among those who might otherwise not even know of their existence. Dissemination of videos over the Internet, to cite just one example, enables terrorists to rely less on traditional news media to deliver their messages to widespread audiences. Online proselytizing is particularly useful in capturing the interest of potential "lone-wolf" terrorists who might launch attacks without having any real ties to Al Qaeda or other terrorist organizations.[53]

On a more conventional level, governments around the world are surely taking note of the importance of new media in the Arab uprisings. The Internet is particularly susceptible to "false flag" operations that can be used to disseminate disinformation or entrap dissidents. As social media become more widely used for political tasks, these problems will require increasing attention because media users will become more sophisticated, developing and employing their own tricks of the trade. In Sudan in early 2011, authorities used Facebook and text messages to encourage protestors to gather at a particular place in Khartoum, and then arrested them when they arrived.[54]

Just as governments seeking to stifle dissent can restrict or misuse media, so too can other governments deploy (or withhold) tools to open up media use. During events such as the Arab uprisings, these pros and cons are weighed by those who shape policy. One US State Department official said in January 2011, "None of us are cyberutopians; we have always been clear-eyed about this. The question is not whether tech is good or bad. It's disruptive. And in a disruptive environment the question is, how can you maximize your interests?"[55]

After all, maximizing one's interests is the essence of foreign policy, and governments are increasingly alert to ways that new media affect this process.

Reverberations

Aside from their use in intense political activity, as in the Arab uprisings, social media are becoming more common as parts of the social and cultural fabrics of nations, cultures, and religions. An example is the Pakistan-based millatfacebook.com, which was created in response to a Facebook page calling for an "Everybody Draw Mohammed Day." Drawings purported to be of the Prophet Mohammed are considered blasphemous by Muslims, and this Facebook posting led a judge in Pakistan to ban Facebook, Twitter, Google, YouTube, and other sites.

Millatfacebook, which is actually a website, not a Facebook page, states that its objective is "to provide a platform for all Muslims and nice, decent and sophisticated people of all religions and faiths, to come together and make a network. They should interact in a way that is socially responsible by providing them all the freedom of expression, however respecting each other's sentiments, sensitivities and beliefs."[56] (*Millat* is the Urdu equivalent of the Arabic *ummah*, meaning the global community of Islam.) A more combative rationale for the site was offered by Usman Zaheer, the chief operating officer of the software house that hosts Millatfacebook, who said: "We want to tell Facebook people if they mess with us they have to face the consequences. If someone commits blasphemy against our Prophet Mohammed then we will become his competitor and give him immense business loss."[57]

In Pakistan, as in other developing countries, the access to such sites—and access to new media generally—is in practice limited to urban elites due to a combination of widespread illiteracy and the still scattered availability of the Internet. As new media slowly build their audience in Pakistan, the country's volatility makes the effects of expanded media access both significant and hard to predict. Poverty, political frustration, and a median age of 21 make Pakistan similar in many ways to the Arab countries in which uprisings occurred in 2011. This has led some Pakistani political analysts to predict their country's own explosion, and media could be a factor in the timing and extent of that detonation.[58]

Perhaps the most interesting long-distance response to the Arab Awakening has come from China, which although an emerging great power is so insecure in that status that it responds in heavy-handed ways to perceived threats to its political stability.

As of June 2011, more than 485 million Chinese were using the Internet, slightly more than a third of the population, with another 5 million users in Hong Kong and Macao.[59] Those numbers have made the Chinese government wary of online media's current and prospective impact. In February 2011, when an anonymous online appeal called for "Jasmine Revolution" protests in Beijing, Shanghai, and 11 other Chinese cities, the government deployed more police than there were protestors, and the revolution, at least for the moment, receded. Zhou Yongkang, China's domestic security chief and a member of the Communist Party's Politburo Standing Committee, the country's top decision-making body, called on officials to "strive to defuse conflicts and disputes while they are still embryonic." At about the same time, President Hu Jintao called for tighter supervision of the Internet in order to prevent unrest, and another party official told journalists: "We're not afraid. We don't have anything to worry about, but we have to prevent people from using the Internet to damage or destroy social stability." He compared the Internet to a nuclear weapon in that it could make the country strong but also expose it to new dangers.[60]

For a government that was "not afraid," the reaction was remarkably severe. James Fallows called it "the most serious and widespread wave of repression since the Tiananmen Square crackdowns" in 1989. He wrote that human rights lawyers were arrested or detained (often placed under house arrest), and then the activists who were their clients began to disappear. The Chinese artist and activist Ai Weiwei, who had 96,000 followers on Twitter, was among those detained.[61]

The Chinese news media had delayed in reporting the Arab uprisings, but when they finally did so the coverage stressed the chaotic nature of events there. The official line was to show no sympathy for those who might foster similar upheaval in China. One newspaper, commenting on Western objections to the treatment of Ai Weiwei, stated, "The West's behavior aims at disrupting the attention of Chinese society and attempts to modify the value system of the Chinese people."[62]

China closed the Internet in Xinjiang province in 2009 when ethnic riots occurred there. Other autocratic states have restricted or shut down Internet access, Nepal and Uganda among them.[63] Other governments close particular sites or services when they feel threatened or even just annoyed, and as online usage extends into underdeveloped autocratic countries, cyber repression is likely to increase. The OpenNet Initiative (http://opennet.net) monitors Internet censorship and surveillance and has new items to report almost every day. Openness is neither easily won nor easily retained.

★   ★   ★

A concluding point about China is this: the government has learned to act quickly, recognizing how fast a protest movement can come together using social media as an organizational tool. Events in the Arab world in 2011 have reinforced Chinese resolve to control online politics. This might not be "real-time diplomacy," but it is real-time political policing. Chinese officials may even realize that they are overreacting in some cases, but they know that if protests gain traction, they will be much harder to stop.

As with real-time diplomacy, the internal political affairs of nations are being reshaped by the speed and pervasiveness of new media. The next chapters will examine how this directly affects the processes of foreign policy.

PART II

DIPLOMACY TURNED
UPSIDE-DOWN

CHAPTER 3

TRADITIONAL DIPLOMACY AND THE CUSHION OF TIME

Events have always moved quickly, but until recently information about these events arrived more slowly. Governments usually first found out what was happening from their own suppliers of information—diplomats, the military, intelligence agencies, and other proprietary sources. The public depended on the news media, which often had to transmit information through mechanisms slower and less reliable than those available to governments.

This has changed within the past half-century, as new communications technology has fostered a temporal parity between the occurrence and the reporting of events. News organizations and, more recently, "citizen journalists" have outpaced other information providers, including those on which governments have traditionally relied. Policymakers now look to these diverse, public news purveyors as essential tools for creating a picture of what is going on in the world. Speed of delivery, however, is not always matched by reliability of content.

To understand how acceleration of the information flow has changed foreign policy decision making, studying some cases from the past might be helpful.

When Events Outpaced
News Coverage

During the early morning hours of Sunday, August 13, 1961, East German forces shut down the border between East and West Berlin. It began with barbed wire and fencing. Soon thereafter, it became "The Wall."

Reporter Daniel Schorr was on the scene. He and his CBS News crew filmed what was taking place and quickly took their film to Berlin's Templehof Airport, where it was put on a propeller plane going to London. From there, after some hours, it was flown by Pan Am to New York, where it was taken to a film-processing lab. Even with the benefit of the time-zone change, it was now Sunday afternoon in the United States, about 16 hours after Schorr had compiled his report. Once CBS editors and producers were done with it, Schorr's story aired on the network's newscast Tuesday night.[1]

Meanwhile, print coverage about events in Berlin was only somewhat timelier. The first story appeared as a last-minute addition to the Sunday, August 13 edition of the *New York Times*—an article from Reuters with a Berlin dateline, headlined, "Commuting Ended: Warsaw Pact States Say Allies' Routes Remain Open." The lead was simply, "East Germany closed the border early today between East and West Berlin," and the story went on to say that East German troops were standing guard at the Brandenburg Gate, the main crossing point in the city. It noted that the flow of refugees through West Berlin had recently averaged 1,700 each day. The article quoted at length from a statement issued by the Warsaw Pact, but cited no American or other Western official response.[2]

By the following day, the *Times* had its own reporters on the story. Harry Gilroy's report from Berlin, "Mood of Berlin: Controlled Fury," ran under a four-column headline: "Soviet Troops Encircle Berlin To Back Up Sealing of Border; U.S. Is Drafting Vigorous Protest." Reporting from Moscow, Seymour Topping wrote a story headlined "Closing of Border Is Seen as First of Soviet Moves." In neither of these articles was a US official quoted. The *Times* printed the lengthy Warsaw Pact statement and East German decree, and the text of a statement issued by Secretary of State Dean Rusk assailing the Communists' action and stating that "these violations of existing agreements will be the subject of vigorous protest through appropriate channels."[3]

On its editorial page on Monday, 14, the *Times* stated: "The new armed ring set up between West and East Berlin is intended as a test of the free world. Will the United States and its allies dare do anything besides send oral and written protests as the Soviet Union unilaterally violates past solemn commitments?"[4] In another editorial the following day, the *Times* said: "After hurling bloodcurdling threats of atomic annihilation against anyone interfering with his designs on Berlin and Germany, Premier Khrushchev is now making his first real test of the Western will to resist force and lead him to the conference table.... But President Kennedy, with the support of our allies, has solemnly proclaimed our determination to defend the freedom of West Berlin."[5]

American news organizations were following the story as it developed, but the tone of the reporting was not alarmist. This relatively soft coverage was the media backdrop against which President John F. Kennedy was to shape his response. Vacationing in Hyannis Port, Massachusetts, he had been informed about events in Berlin late Sunday morning, , more than 12 hours after the barricades began being set up in Berlin. Officials at the State and Defense Departments had delayed contacting the president partly because they were perplexed about what the East Germans were up to. US policy options had been based on the assumption that any blockading undertaken by the Communists in Berlin would be to seal off access to West Berlin, but Allied routes into the city were unimpeded. After the State Department Operations Center sent a telex to the president, Secretary of State Rusk called him. Following their conversation, Kennedy determined that there was no immediate threat to American interests or personnel and so he decided to take no immediate action. The president went sailing, and Rusk went to a Washington Senators baseball game.[6]

The apparently relaxed response of the president was a signal to the Kremlin that the United States was not going to react rashly and that the "crisis" was not going to escalate. The president's low-key reaction also bought time for more information to be gathered. Despite newspaper headlines such as those of the *Times* on Monday, interest in the events in Berlin remained low on the news agenda. At the Monday morning White House press briefing, press secretary Pierre Salinger was not queried about Berlin until after 34 questions about other topics had been asked.[7] Even as late as Wednesday, August 16, few Kennedy administration officials were being quoted for attribution. Max Frankel's story in the *Times* said the administration was painting the Berlin move as "a dramatic confession of Communist failure," and he cited "the highest officials" as saying that "protest and vigorous propaganda will be their primary form of retaliation." The highest-ranking official quoted in the story was

Under Secretary of State Chester Bowles, who gave a speech in Washington addressing Berlin issues.[8]

By the time the Schorr's news footage of the first barricades aired on the 15th, US policymakers had a better sense of what Soviet and East German intentions were, and they were not inclined to treat the Berlin wall-building as a major Soviet policy shift requiring a provocative military response (although many citizens of West Berlin may have felt otherwise). As Kennedy aide Theodore Sorensen observed, "Not one responsible official—in this country, in West Berlin, West Germany or Western Europe—suggested that Allied forces should march into East German territory and tear the Wall down. . . . Nor did any ally or adviser want an excited Western response that might trigger an uprising among the desperate East Berliners that would only produce another Budapest massacre."[9]

The Wall remained a symbol of Communist oppression for 28 years and Berlin was a tense hot spot for much of that time, but in retrospect the measured American reaction seems wise.

Consider how the scenario might have been different had today's communication apparatus been available in August 1961. Daniel Schorr's CBS team would not have been worried about getting their film to the airport; they would have been on the air live throughout the early morning hours in Berlin (which were in the midst of prime-time in the United States) and they would have had plenty of company, as the full array of national and global satellite news companies would have been there with them on the scene. YouTube would feature hundreds of videos taken by spectators, Twitter would flash terse reports from onlookers, and cell phone video would attract followers to Facebook's own walls. Some of these reports would be sent from residents of East Berlin. All this "breaking news" would be delivered in a steady stream, punctuated by dramatic commentary from television anchors and with minimal context related to larger geopolitical issues.

How would President Kennedy have responded in those circumstances? Would he have gone sailing or would he have rushed back to Washington as his advisors developed a media strategy for the crisis? Rolling some US tanks up to the boundary line might make for good video and might be reassuring to Americans made nervous by the alarmist news reports they were receiving about the latest Communist perfidy. The president might decide he needed to go on television himself and challenge Soviet Premier Nikita Khrushchev's tactics. Had that been the case, what would the Soviets and their East German allies have then done?

Perhaps Kennedy would have been as restrained in his response in this hypothetical situation as he was in reality, but he would have faced far different pressures due to the speed at which information moved. Like the general public, he would have a large amount of information at his disposal, but with little ability to judge the accuracy of much of it.

In dealing with the 1961 Berlin crisis, Kennedy was one of the last presidents to enjoy a pace that should not be called leisurely, but certainly was not frantic. His successors found themselves first facing increasingly influential live television coverage and then the array of newer media. This growth in the supply of information changed the political environment in which presidential decisions were made.

Senior US foreign policy officials had long recognized the importance of managing the time pressures that affected their work. Dean Acheson wrote that Harry Truman's judgment during the early days of his presidency was "inclined to be hasty as though pushed out by the pressure of responsibility, and perhaps also by concern that deliberateness might seem indecisiveness." Acheson then added approvingly: "But he learned fast and soon would ask, 'How long have we got to work this out?' He would take what time was available for study and then decide."[10]

In praising some diplomats from an earlier era, George Kennan observed that they were "men so measured and prudent in their judgment of others, so careful to reserve that judgment until they felt they had the facts, [and] so well aware of the danger of inadequate evidence and hasty conclusion..." Kennan also explained his concern about the executive branch feeling itself "beholden to short-term trends of public opinion," and "the erratic and subjective nature of public reaction to foreign-policy questions." He added, "I do not consider public reaction to foreign-policy questions to be erratic and undependable over the long term; but I think the record indicates that in the short term our public opinion, or what passes for our public opinion in the thinking of official Washington, can be easily led astray into areas of emotionalism and subjectivity which make it a poor and inadequate guide for national action."[11]

Kennan wrote this in 1951, and throughout the next half-century he warned repeatedly about the dangers of allowing emotionalism to infect foreign policy. In these later writings he sometimes focused on media influence, particularly what he considered to be the pernicious effects of television coverage on decision making. In December 1992, after watching the televised landing of US troops in Somalia, Kennan wrote that the reason for Congress and the American public supporting the intervention "lies primarily with the exposure of the Somalia situation by the American media; above all, television. The reaction would have been unthinkable without this exposure." He added, "But if American policy from here on out, particularly policy involving the uses of our armed forces abroad, is to be controlled by popular emotional impulses, and especially ones provoked by the commercial television industry, then there is no place not only for myself, but for the responsible deliberative organs of our government, in both executive and legislative branches."[12]

Kennan's observations had a valedictory tone; he was 88 years old at the time (he lived to be 101), and his observations illustrate the generational differences among policymakers. Kennan could not imagine letting television drive policy, while officials in the George H. W. Bush and Bill Clinton administrations who were making Somalia-related decisions presumably could not imagine a policy that was not at least partially shaped—at least in terms of winning public support—by television. Some would argue that Kennan held an elitist view of foreign policymaking, wishing it was still the exclusive domain of people like him. Whether that would be a good or bad thing is open to question, but the late-twentieth century-rise of new media technologies had a democratizing influence on diplomacy because more people were aware of world events and this resulted in popular political pressure that policymakers recognized.

At about this time, policymakers were also learning that real-time news coverage could take on a life of its own, regardless of what was actually happening among diplomats. Secretary of State James A. Baker, when engaged in talks with Iraqi foreign minister Tariq Aziz in early 1991 in an effort to avoid war over Iraq's invasion of Kuwait, observed that when the discussions lasted longer than expected, there were "rumors of a diplomatic breakthrough we knew were baseless but powerless to suppress. World financial markets and oil prices gyrated wildly as CNN fed the proceedings live throughout the globe. It was a bizarre way to conduct diplomacy, but unavoidable in an era of instant telecommunications."[13]

During these same talks with Aziz, Baker presented a short briefing to the news media, which reflected Baker's pessimistic view of prospects for a peaceful resolution of the dispute and was carried live throughout the world. When he began speaking, the price of oil was US$23.35 a barrel; five minutes later it was US$31.[14]

By the early 1990s, what Baker called a "bizarre way to conduct diplomacy" had become the norm. Diplomats had learned that CNN and its media siblings were significant players in the diplomatic process, generating ripple effects such as those Baker noted. The rapidity of these effects continues to accelerate, driven by technology, but it is worth noting that time pressure, in one form or another, has always been part of diplomacy and that an appreciation of precedent is always useful.

Nothing Is New

America 1775

During the morning of April 19, 1775, American militiamen and British army regulars faced off at Lexington and Concord, Massachusetts, in bloody confrontations that marked the beginning of the American Revolution. After the British soldiers made their way back to Boston, leaders of the rebellion needed to spread word of events as quickly as possible to the other American colonies. Historian David Hackett Fischer charted the progress of the news: It reached Providence, Rhode Island, that night and New London, Connecticut, the following night; a report reached New York City late on April 23 and Philadelphia on the 24th; an express rider delivered a handbill describing the events to Annapolis, Maryland, on April 26; the story reached Williamsburg, Virginia, on the 28th; a ship brought the news to Charleston, South Carolina, on May 9; and settlers in western Pennsylvania also learned about the clashes in early May.[15]

Meanwhile, proponents of American independence raced to deliver their version of events—eyewitness testimonies, copies of the *Salem* (Massachusetts) *Gazette* carrying reports of the battles, and a letter written by Dr. Joseph Warren of the Massachusetts

Committee of Safety—to the British public before British General Thomas Gage's dispatch could reach London. With British opinion split about how to deal with the American colonies, the Americans hoped to sway the British public and government with their report. The American version of events declared that the British troops had been the first to open fire and that this had been evidence of premeditated "ministerial vengeance against this colony."[16]

The voyage across the Atlantic often took six weeks, but the Americans' vessel, stripped of cargo, made it in 30 days, beating Gage's report by two weeks. A notice was placed in a London newspaper stating that the report from Massachusetts was available to be read in the office of the lord mayor of London. British newspapers picked up the story; one decried the "cruel and inhuman proceedings" of the British army, stating that the soldiers' conduct had "as never before disgraced the character of British soldiery."[17]

By entrusting his report to a ship that was ill-suited for express delivery, even in the context of Atlantic crossings at that time, Gage had allowed an information vacuum to exist in London and the Americans gladly filled it. With no official report to counteract the Americans' message, the British government found itself under intense pressure by the less-hawkish factions in the debate about what to do concerning the American colonies. In the end, however, it made little difference, and the American Revolution became a full-scale conflict.

This case illustrates what can happen when information is available from just a few sources and with considerable disparity in the times of delivery. Those in King George III's government who were trying to manage public and parliamentary opinion about the situation in the colonies had to operate under a handicap until the arrival of the ship carrying Gage's report. Further, by reflecting the opposite of the modern situation—in which so much information is available so quickly—this case underscores the value of information per se and the significance of speed, as well as the relationship between the two.

Then as now, those on two sides of a political conflict each wanted to get their versions of events delivered to a distant audience as quickly as possible. Those who were required to make policy decisions found themselves vulnerable because one of those sides, in this instance the Americans, was able to use speed to ensure that its favorably one-sided narrative would be unchallenged while initial public opinion took shape.

Great Britain 1940

In the eighteenth century, dispatches about events that had occurred weeks (or longer) before were avidly read as "breaking news" bulletins. There was no alternative. The following century saw the telegraph and then the telephone come into use, and by the first half of the twentieth century, communication technology was evolving with remarkable speed.

Radio had transformative effect on the flow and absorption of information. In the United States in 1921, 60,000 homes had radios and there were 30 radio stations in the entire country. By 1940, 29 million American homes (out of a total of 35 million) had radios, and 814 stations were operating around the nation.[18]

Much of the content of radio broadcasts was entertainment, but journalism was also gaining a foothold. Radio news changed the consumption of information in two important ways: first, the major networks—CBS, NBC, and Mutual—were national in their reach, which meant that for the first time on a continuing basis a single news source could have an audience throughout the country; and second, news could be delivered in real time, offering a "you are there" vividness that was unprecedented.

These two factors profoundly influenced the content and effects of news. American journalism had primarily been a localized business, reflecting local interests, customs, standards, prejudices, and other facets of communities ranging from big cities to small towns. This contributed to an informational parochialism in which the big picture mattered mainly as it affected local interests. There were stories that captured national attention: a presidential election, baseball's World Series, international events of great importance (such as wars in which the United States was involved), and such others. Because of the geographical limits imposed by news technology, common information was not often shared nationally, and journalism did not, for the most part, contribute to instilling a sense of nationhood.

Radio changed that. Whether a listener was in New York, a few blocks from a network's headquarters, or 3,000 miles away on the

West Coast, she or he heard the same newscast. That meant that there was intellectual common ground on which anyone with a radio could share the same information. The New Yorker and the Californian were connected.

Political figures soon came to appreciate the advantages of having a national stage. President Franklin D. Roosevelt was an exceptionally adroit radio performer, and he used his "fireside chats" to enter the living rooms of Americans to explain his New Deal and other policies. Demagogues also found radio to be a congenial tool; in the United States, Huey Long and Father Charles Coughlin were the most notorious of these, while in Germany Adolf Hitler used radio to instill fervor in the mass audience.

By the time Britain and France declared war on Germany in 1939, radio news had begun to mature. Radio was primarily an entertainment medium and news was a secondary concern of network executives. NBC relied heavily on newspaper reporters, government officials, and other outsiders to present news; Mutual had a few star newscasters, such as Raymond Gram Swing; and CBS had begun developing its own cadre of correspondents. *Variety* said that CBS's innovative approach offered listeners a "family group" of reporters who were getting "closer to the human element, and they get to essentials quickly, interpret past and present as simply as possible for the ordinary listener."[19]

Rising to the role of paterfamilias of the CBS group was Edward R. Murrow. He had come to Europe as an administrator for the network, and found himself behind a microphone for the first time on a day when no one else was available. Murrow soon became the central figure in CBS's wartime coverage, and he built a team of correspondents—William L. Shirer, Eric Sevareid, Charles Collingwood, and others—who provided Americans with crisp, sophisticated reports from Europe.

Murrow was an innovator. Radio reporters had generally gathered their information, written their scripts, and delivered the news from studios. Murrow did that as well, but he also went into the streets so his listeners could hear Londoners' footsteps as they went about their business following a night of German bombing, and onto the city's rooftops during air raids to give Americans a sense of what it was like to live amidst the sounds of sirens, antiaircraft fire, and explosions. He was the only reporter broadcasting live during air raids—not even British journalists had permission to do so—because Prime Minister Winston Churchill personally approved Murrow's request. Churchill, desperate for increased US involvement in the war, was counting on Murrow's dramatic live reporting to help break down American isolationism. To some extent that happened. The power of Murrow's work was well described in 1941 by Archibald MacLeish: "You burned the city of London in our houses, and we felt the flames that burned it. You laid the dead of London at our doors, and we knew the dead were our dead."[20]

Americans had never heard anything like this. Most were happy to not be involved in yet another European war, but here was Murrow vividly and in real-time coming into their homes from London, telling them about the courageous Brits and evil Nazis and making clear that America would not long remain outside Hitler's plans for conquest. The sirens and explosions sounded so close, within the living room. Murrow was planting seeds of doubt about isolationism, and Franklin Roosevelt—once he secured his reelection in 1940—was ready to harvest the results.

Few presidents have possessed shrewd political judgment comparable to Roosevelt's. He had a remarkable sense of just how far out in front of public opinion he could get before leadership became detachment. He needed Murrow and other American journalists to make a presumably nonpolitical case for intervention—first economic, and then military—on behalf of Britain.

The most convincing way for this case to be made was in the form of news reports, particularly those that dramatically conveyed the harsh reality of Britain under siege. Churchill also understood this dynamic, which is why he ordered that Murrow be allowed on London rooftops and why he so assiduously courted Murrow and other American journalists. The prime minister understood that American voices—not his own or those of the BBC—were most likely to sway American opinion.

This was a case in which political leaders used real-time information to enhance their diplomatic strategy. It is worth noting that it was not the information in itself that was crucial—basically the same reports could be found in newspapers—but rather the intrinsic drama of real-time news. This immediacy captivated listeners and engaged their sympathies. Roosevelt and Churchill watched as American public opinion surveys showed increasing willingness to support Britain. In May 1941, a Gallup survey reflected a striking abandonment of isolationism: 77 percent of respondents said the United States should aid Britain even at the risk of being drawn into the war.[21]

By December 1941, when Pearl Harbor was bombed and the United States entered the war, radio had prepared the American public for this new level of involvement.

Television and the Drama of Foreign Affairs

Murrow understood the power of words and background audio entering homes during the radio generation, and he became one of the first broadcast journalists to effectively use television to present news that went beyond terse headline reports. Television's first war took place in Korea, and in late 1950 and early 1951 Murrow reported from the front lines there, with video of the harsh conditions backing up his words.

By the 1960s, television was becoming an increasingly important element of the culture of the developed world. In the United States, more than 90 percent of households had a television set, and watching TV became an integral part of many lives. Although primarily providing entertainment, television had also become an essential news medium, supplementing (and sometimes displacing) print and radio journalism. In a television-oriented culture, news consumers wanted video as part of their information diet.

As the Vietnam War intensified during the late 1960s, so did its coverage by American television networks. This was the first comprehensively televised war, but the reach of satellite technology was not yet extensive enough to allow live coverage from Vietnam. This meant that television reports often reached the public a day or two later than newspaper stories about the same event, such as a battle, and so television war correspondents were not pressured to deliver "breaking news" as they are today. They could take time to report and analyze thoroughly, something that has become an exception when live coverage is the norm.

This did not, however, reduce the impact of television's treatment of combat news. The nature of television was a factor in itself; how people saw things physically affected how they visualized them intellectually. As President Lyndon Johnson was to painfully learn, this had a significant effect on public opinion about his Vietnam policy.

Johnson was unprepared to deal with the ramifications of presiding over the first "living-room war." This concept was best explained by Michael Arlen, television critic of the *New Yorker* magazine: "We were watching, a bit numbly perhaps (we have watched it so often), real men get shot at, real men (our surrogates, in fact) get killed and wounded."[22]

For a public physically distanced from the war, television reports in the living room replaced newsreels in the movie theater, and the intimacy of war being present within the household was significant, with visual images amplifying the effect that Murrow's London reporting had delivered. In a movie theater, the images on the screen are much larger than life-size, and the person watching them is surrounded by perhaps hundreds of strangers. A visit to a movie theater is, for almost everyone, an occasion that is outside daily routine, so the psychological state of the audience member is not the same as that of someone who flicks on the television set every evening at home.

Perhaps most important is the viewer's acceptance of the people seen on television as being in her or his home. This applies whether the "visitor" is a late-night talk show host, a network news anchor, or a wounded soldier in a newscast. Depending on the size of the television screen, the people seen—especially in a close-up—are almost life-size, not like the giants on the movie theater screen, and as such are like real guests in the home. What happens to those guests—American soldiers, Vietnamese civilians—may capture the attention and the sympathy of the viewer, and that may in turn affect opinion on whether the war is worth fighting.

This is a complicated process that affects different individuals in various ways, but during the 1960s, when the nightly newscasts of the three major networks had massive viewership in the United States, this was something policymakers had to respect and grapple with. This was a challenge because what the viewer saw, in a two-minute report from the war zone, often lacked "big picture" context. As Michael Arlen described the process, Americans looked at stories from Vietnam "as a child kneeling in a corridor, his eye to the keyhole, looks at two grownups arguing in a locked room—the aperture of the keyhole small; the figures shadowy, mostly out of sight; the voices indistinct."[23]

A particularly dramatic story or riveting image might, to the average television viewer, seem to represent the entire war and contribute to shaping that person's political behavior, including how to vote in the next election. Policymakers during the Vietnam era may have first dismissed television coverage as too superficial to have lasting effect, but as public opposition to the war grew, they changed their minds, recognizing its impact. Finally, when the war was lost, many of the military and civilians who had defined war policy blamed defeat on "the media," which they felt had provided inaccurate coverage that fueled the antiwar movement and broader public dissatisfaction.

The notion that the press "lost the war" was and remains nonsense. One of the wiser officials at the time, Clark Clifford, who was secretary of defense during the final two years of the Johnson presidency, later wrote: "Reporters and the antiwar movement did not defeat America in Vietnam. Our policy failed because it was based on false premises and false promises. Had the results in Vietnam approached, even remotely, what Washington and Saigon had publicly predicted for many years, the American people would have continued to support their government."[24]

Lyndon Johnson and later Richard Nixon learned that television created constraints on policymaking because people could see for themselves what was happening on the ground in the war zone. Political leaders could no longer simply say that journalists had gotten the story wrong, because the public was seeing the story, even if often with just the "keyhole" view that Arlen described. Sometimes emotion about the news of the moment superseded logic-based assessment of the overall status of the war.

Further, the speed with which information was delivered to the public was increasing, meaning that policymakers had to pick up their own pace if they were to respond in timely fashion to news reports. Johnson was so intent on staying ahead of the news media that he had a wire service news ticker and several television sets installed in the Oval Office.

The influence of the news media to shape public opinion about the war could be seen in the aftermath of the Tet offensive in 1968. The Vietnamese Communists had thrown 70,000 troops into battle and had inflicted heavy casualties on US forces: more than 500 Americans killed and 2,500 wounded in one week.

Nevertheless, military historians today overwhelmingly agree that Tet proved to be a serious defeat for the Vietnamese Communist forces. They suffered heavy casualties, were unable to hold the cities they had attacked, and failed to stir up a popular uprising against the South Vietnamese government. But at the time, the American news media pronounced Tet to be a major setback for the United States. Part of this was due to the overly optimistic projections by the administration (as cited by Clark Clifford) that had preceded the offensive. Many journalists thought they had been lied to consistently by the administration, and they seized upon this opportunity to expose those lies. Political communication scholar Daniel Hallin wrote: "The journalists were inescapably a part of the political process they were reporting. If they said Tet was a political defeat for the Administration, they were helping to make it so; if they resisted the journalistic instinct to put Tet in that context, they were helping the Administration out. Most of them followed that journalistic instinct."[25]

The post-Tet journalistic pronouncement with the most profound effect on the administration's Vietnam policy came from CBS News anchor Walter Cronkite. Wearing a helmet and flak jacket, Cronkite presented a special "Report from Vietnam by Walter Cronkite" (i.e., not part of his nightly newscast) that showed him at the scene of the Tet battlegrounds. He wrapped up his report from his anchor desk in the New York newsroom offering this analysis: "To say that we are mired in stalemate seems the only realistic, yet unsatisfactory conclusion. On the off chance that the military and political analysts are right, in the next months we must test the enemy's intentions in case this is indeed his last big gasp before negotiations. But it is increasingly clear to this reporter that the only rational way out then will be to negotiate, not as victors but as an honorable people who lived up to their pledge to defend democracy, and did the best they could."[26]

"Not as victors" ran directly against the stream of optimistic statements the administration had been issuing for years. Coming from Cronkite—billed, probably correctly, as "the most trusted man in America"—this had devastating impact. In some ways Cronkite looked more presidential than the president; his viewers could see him in the field in Vietnam and then in the magisterial anchor's chair. President Johnson told his press secretary, George Christian, that Cronkite would change the minds of "middle-of-the-road folks who have supported the war all along."[27]

In his memoirs, Johnson said: "There was a great deal of emotional and exaggerated reporting of the Tet offensive in our press and on television. The media seemed to be in competition as to who could provide the most lurid and depressing accounts.... The American people and even a number of officials in government, subjected to this daily barrage of bleakness and near panic, began to think we must have suffered a defeat."[28]

Johnson was particularly sensitive to television coverage and how it affected policy. On the day after he declared he would not seek reelection in 1968, Johnson spoke to the National Association of Broadcasters about this: "As I sat in my office last evening, waiting to speak, I thought of the many times each week when television brings the war into the American home. No one can say exactly what effect those vivid scenes would have on American opinion. Historians must only guess at the effect that television would have had during earlier conflicts on the future of this nation: during the Korean War, for example, at that time when our forces were pushed back there to Pusan; or World War II, the Battle of the Bulge, or when our men were slugging it out in Europe."[29]

Johnson's posing these historical hypothetical questions is intriguing because it reflects his frustration about being at the mercy of images. He was a master of old-fashioned political power, which he had wielded with great success as an arm-twister in the US Senate, and he had won a landslide victory in the presidential election of 1964. But as the first president to feel the political sting that television coverage of a war could deliver, Johnson never understood the need to add a media-sensitive dimension to the exercise of power so he could respond to the video stories from Vietnam that often seemed to dramatically contradict the administration's version of what was happening there.

Johnson's failure to comprehend the ways that the new media of the time could constrain policymaking was understandable. Television's breakthrough political moment had happened relatively recently—the televised debates between John Kennedy and Richard Nixon during the 1960 presidential campaign—and only gradually was recognition growing about how television was altering individuals' relationship with the larger world.

The "global village" that Marshall McLuhan had described in the early 1960s was taking shape in ways that brought distant wars and other international events into people's media-defined neighborhoods. The connection was virtual; no blood from a television news story would spill onto the living-room rug and so some emotional distance could be maintained. This was, however, part of a reordering of geopolitics that diplomats, like other officials, needed to accept and adjust to.

Moving into Real Time

On January 17, 1991, the United States started its bombardment of Baghdad as the beginning of Operation Desert Storm, also known as the Gulf War, which by mid-April had liberated Kuwait from invading Iraqi forces. Among the notable aspects of this war was television's role, which was considerably different from that which it had played in Vietnam. In this conflict, the hallmark of the television reporting was the real-time coverage that new satellite broadcasting technology allowed.

At the time, CNN was the leader in live, global coverage. Founded by Ted Turner in 1980, CNN was America's first 24-hour all-news channel, providing news to the viewers when *they* wanted it rather than their being at the mercy of a network's schedule. By 1991, it provided news to more than 100 countries, and was relied upon by governments to supplement their own flows of information from intelligence and diplomatic channels. When President George H. W. Bush ordered that Iraq be attacked, he could not do so in advance in a television address to the American public because he knew that the Iraqi leadership would see it at the same time. He needed to wait until the attack was underway and the world had already found out about it through live news reports. This was just one example of how CNN and its siblings would affect how governments and their leaders reshaped their approaches to international politics in the global television era.

CNN's diplomatic role included serving as a messenger medium. When direct communication between US and Iraqi officials broke down, either side could talk on CNN's air and be certain that the other side would see it. CNN chairman Ted Turner recognized the network's importance: "We're a global network. If there's a chance for peace...it might come through us. Hell, both sides aren't talking to each other, but they're talking to CNN. We have a major responsibility."[30] Presumably, this messenger service was the primary reason that Saddam Hussein allowed CNN to remain in Baghdad when other Western news organizations were expelled. He knew that if he should want to reach George Bush quickly, the best way to do so would be through CNN rather than traditional diplomatic mechanisms.

US officials also used CNN to carry messages. Lieutenant General Thomas Kelly, who conducted the Pentagon's press briefings, said after the war that "Every single time I mentioned the use of chemical weapons in a press briefing, I would look into the camera and say, 'You must understand, any commander who uses chemical weapons is going to be held accountable for his actions.' I knew they watched CNN in Iraq, and I wanted those guys to hear that."[31]

In terms of journalistic quality, live coverage from a war zone could be deeply flawed. During the Gulf War, Iraq launched missile attacks against Israel, which were covered live. Lawrence Grossman, a former NBC News president, observed that television viewers were seeing just the "illusion of news" because "the on-the-scene cameras and live satellite pictures at times served to mask reality rather than shed light on what was happening." He added, "Rumors, gossip, speculation, hearsay and unchecked claims were televised live, without verification, without sources, without editing, while we watched newsmen scrambling for gas masks and reacting to missile alerts." Further, wrote Grossman: "In their impatience to get on the air live rather than wait to find out what was going on, television reporters wondered aloud on-screen about what they were seeing and what was happening. No longer did they perform as reporters trying to filter out true information from false. Instead, they were merely sideline observers, as ill-informed as the rest of us. Was it the sound of 'thunder,' or a 'lethal rocket attack' outside? Was it the odor of 'nerve gas' or 'conventional explosives' that was seeping into the TV studio in Tel Aviv? (It turned out to be bus exhaust.)"[32]

Media critics have plenty of fuel for commentary about such matters, but policymakers also must deal with journalism that violates the old rule, "Get it first, but first get it right." Often, what is "right" is a matter of interpretation. Many government officials consider any news report to be "wrong" if it is critical or even merely unpleasant. For them, "good journalism" is coverage that provides political comfort.

Beyond such concerns, however, are matters of substance. That the news media sometimes make mistakes, as was seen in the Tet coverage, is nothing new. But when the traditional news media are supplemented by a large number of online information providers, errors (some unintentional, some purposeful) become more likely and they can have lethal effect. Reports about US involvement in the 1979 attack on the Grand Mosque in Mecca, which were totally untrue, led to an attack on the US embassy in Islamabad, Pakistan, in which seven persons were killed. Many people trust "news" that they are predisposed to believe and respond to it far too quickly for contradictory information to be provided and considered. Again, this in itself is not new, but it happens much faster and more pervasively in the new information era.

Dramatic events in world affairs are often chaotic, and this is reflected in live coverage. Members of the news audience must, to a degree, interpret for themselves what is happening, which means they have a responsibility—often neglected—to educate themselves about the background of current affairs. During the protests in Beijing's Tiananmen Square in 1989, the montage of images that appeared on television showed the disjointed nature of reality. *New York Times* television critic Walter Goodman wrote: "Beginning Saturday night and resuming Sunday morning, the networks had been running still photographs and televised scenes from China as they came in. They conveyed action, confusion, crisis. What exactly was going on was not always clear, but that in a way added to their immediacy. Taken together they told a strong story—soldiers, so many soldiers, moving in on the protesters; students pounding with sticks on an armored troop carrier; burned-out buses and stranded bicycles; the improvised barricades crushed by the military machines; recorded voices of witnesses describing beatings of students by the soldiers."[33]

In this case, television became part of the story. When the Chinese government ordered a halt to live television transmissions, President Bush issued a formal protest on CNN about the events he had been witnessing on CNN.[34] Both CNN and CBS broadcast their own shutdown being ordered by Chinese officials who were "embarrassed and clearly aware they were losing face on live television."[35]

★   ★   ★

Emerging from all these case histories is evidence of a trend toward greater recognition by policymakers of media's role in international affairs and an appreciation of the acceleration of the information process. The pressures related to real-time information flow have, in most instances, replaced the cushion of time that diplomats were accustomed to rely on in earlier days.

Policymakers today are not compelled to act precipitously, but nevertheless they face pressures to move quickly, acknowledging, if not matching, the pace set by the communication technologies that deliver information. They need to have systems in place to sort through the material that pours in and they must push back against media-driven public expectations that all problems can be resolved at the same high speed with which information is provided.

The era in which diplomats talked only to diplomats and scheduled those conversations at their leisure is long past. This is a new time, and new diplomatic practices must be developed that can succeed in the real-time era.

CHAPTER 4

THE ARRIVAL OF
RAPID-REACTION DIPLOMACY

If allowed to do so, passion will influence policy. Rarely, if ever, is that wise. Passion has a way of reshaping truth to serve its purposes, creating traps for those who govern.

An election is stolen; thousands are being gunned down in the streets; millions are demonstrating; the government is about to topple. There may be much truth, or only a little bit, in those allegations, but with the most lurid charges now amplified by new media, they become more credible as they rocket around the world, and there is little that policymakers can do to slow them down, much less negate them. Their existence, however, does not mean that policy should be chained to them. A challenge facing today's diplomats is to find ways to blend speed with wisdom. Good luck.

Iran 2009

The Iranian uprising of 2009 provided a taste of what was to come in the Arab world two years later. People took to the streets against a repressive regime, using social media to aid their mobilization. They talked of freedom, democracy, and fairness in public life. They demanded an end to rigged elections that benefitted only those who were controlled by the bosses of Iranian politics, the mullahs who were accountable to no one..

The outcome was, however, unlike the early victories that were to come in the 2011 Arab Spring. The government of Mahmoud Ahmadinejad was ruthlessly tenacious and had no intention of relinquishing its hold on power. With the backing of the religious leadership and, apparently, the armed forces, it fought back, unleashing its riot police and paramilitary Basij troopers who possessed the numbers and ferocity needed to wear down the protestors.

Dynamics of an Uprising

This was far from being a unique event; it was in the tradition of uprisings in Hungary in 1956, Czechoslovakia in 1968, and others, although there was no external devil, such as the Soviet Union, that could ultimately determine the outcome. Iran's "Green Revolution" (named after the election campaign color of Ahmadinejad's principal rival, Mir-Hossein Mousavi) relied heavily on social media as a mobilization tool, and was the first to be watched by the rest of the world through an array of new media.

On the surface, the demonstrations in Iran were the product of an election that appeared to many to have been rigged. President Ahmadinejad was unpopular in some quarters (many of which were outside Iran) because of policies that had damaged the country's economy and because his sometimes erratic behavior had pushed Iran outside the circle of significant world powers. A close election had been expected, at least according to the international news media, but on June 12 Ahmadinejad received 64 percent of the vote, while Mousavi received 34 percent. Two lesser but still significant candidates received next to nothing.

This outcome was greeted with disbelief, particularly when reports surfaced about Ahmadinejad receiving more votes than there were voters in some places, and when his opponents, who had been strong vote-getters in the past, found themselves with vote totals that made no demographic sense. Runner-up Mousavi called the results a "dangerous charade" and said, "Today, the people's will has been faced with an amazing incidence of lies, hypocrisy, and fraud."[1] Nevertheless, the most powerful person in Iran, Supreme Leader Ayatollah Ali Khamenei, endorsed Ahmadinejad's victory, calling it a "divine assessment."

Although the legitimacy of the vote remains suspect, often overlooked are the preelection surveys conducted for Western news and polling organizations (including the BBC, World Public Opinion, and the University of Maryland), all of which indicated that Ahmadinejad would win by a substantial margin. Numerous Iranian polls had widely varied results, some showing either Ahmadinejad or Mousavi winning by a large margin and others showing a close race. Whatever the validity of any or all of these surveys, it is not at all clear that the election was stolen by Ahmadinejad, whose political appeal—particularly among lower-income and rural Iranians—should not be dismissed.

In retrospect, when comparing Iran 2009 with Tunisia and Egypt 2011, some lessons about modern revolutions emerge. First is that the loyalty of the military, the police, and paramilitary groups will probably be determinative. If they fight back effectively, as was the case with the Basij and police in Iran, they can break the momentum of revolution. In Tunisia and Egypt, the armed forces made clear that they would not take drastic action to crush the revolutions there, and without the regular military the police could not hold back the tide of protest.

Second, momentum is important, and if it can be stalled, the basic strengths of those holding power become even more significant. A revolution must race to reach the finish line—regime change or significant reforms—or else those in power will regroup and the revolution will be in growing danger of failing. In Tunisia and Egypt, the revolutionary public expanded rapidly while the uprisings proceeded quickly, and the governments were never able to buy time by slowing the protestors' efforts. In Iran, the government had enough force at its disposal to block the way to the finish line.

Force trumps fervor. However heroic the revolutionaries may seem, and whatever echoes of *Les Miserables* may be heard by distant audiences, most revolutions can be crushed by timely, organized, and ruthless resistance. Iran 2009 was evidence of that.

Twitter to the Rescue

Twitter in many ways symbolizes (or is symptomatic of) a world in which people are constantly "connecting" with each other, even—or particularly—when they don't have much to say. By limiting messages to 140 characters, Twitter appeals to people who want to communicate but don't want to spend much time doing so.

Born in 2006, Twitter had 400,000 Tweets (messages) posted per quarter in 2007. By mid-2010, the number had risen to 65 million per day. Although Tweets themselves must be brief, they may include links to websites, YouTube, and other information sources. In some ways, it is a more sophisticated, online version of text messaging (SMS), easily usable on cell phones as well as regular computers.

In 2009, Twitter's universal question to its users changed from "What are you doing?" to "What's happening?" This shift helped bring Twitter into a more public, reportorial role. This was exemplified by the use of Twitter during the terrorist attacks in Mumbai in 2008. People on the scene, including some who were in the hotels seized by the terrorists, sent Tweets at an estimated rate of 70 every five seconds, providing reports of what was happening, asking for blood donors to come to a local hospital, and letting family members know that they were safe.[2] One witness who reported steadily on Twitter said, "I felt I had a responsibility to share my view with the outside world."[3]

Twitter also attracted attention during April 2009, when protestors in Moldova reportedly used Tweets to help organize street demonstrations against election results that favored the Communist Party. Some international news organizations were quick to proclaim that a "Twitter revolution" was underway. But as attractive a formulation as that may be, it is flawed:

- There appeared to be very few Twitter users in Moldova.
- The government shut down cell phone service, so the main square where the demonstrations took place was a communication dead zone. (One observer said the communication tool that would have been most useful there was a megaphone.)
- Most of the Tweets about the events in Moldova came from outside the country, which was useful for attracting international attention to events there, but had little effect on the demonstrations themselves.[4] One study found that of 700 persons Tweeting about the Moldovan protests, fewer than 200 were inside the country.[5]

The bona fides of some of the participants in the Moldovan demonstrations were also questioned, with suspicions that government provocateurs had instigated the violence and had placed a Romanian flag on the Presidency building in order to discredit Moldova's political opposition.[6]

In other words, Tweets do not make a revolution. At least part of the reason political ferment is ascribed to Twitter, Facebook, and other such tools may be that they are Western inventions, and Western policymakers and publics would like to see their stamp on revolutions that they approve of. This parochialism and wishful thinking distorts reality, overrating the role of fashionable media tools. This is a factor that has appeared throughout the brief history of these new media venues, and this outlook must be corrected if the real politics of change are to be understood.

This is not to say that Twitter is useless. It can be used on the run and its messages are easy to group by topic and spread to a global audience. But, as *Time* magazine's Lev Grossman observed while the Iranian protests were taking place, "As is so often the case in the media world, Twitter's strengths are also its weaknesses. The vast body of information about current events in Iran that circulates on Twitter is chaotic, subjective, and totally unverifiable. It's impossible to authenticate sources. It's also not clear who exactly is using Twitter within Iran, especially in English. Anecdotal evidence suggests that the bulk of tweets are coming from 'hyphenated' Iranians not actually in the country who are getting the word out to Western observers, rather than from the protestors themselves, who favor other, less public media. This is, after all, a country where the government once debated the death penalty for dissident bloggers."[7]

That is a good summary of the uncertainties surrounding the role of Twitter and other social media in Iran and elsewhere. Certainly new media have considerable appeal in Iran, where a third of the population is younger than 30. In 2009, out of a national population of about 77 million, more than 23 million Iranians (30 percent) had Internet access, more than 45 million (58 percent) had mobile phones, and more than 110,000 blogs had appeared.[8]

As the postelection demonstrations gained strength in Iran, the US government wanted to be certain that the protest movement had access to Twitter for internal communication and to let the rest of the world know what was going on. State Department official Jared Cohen contacted Twitter to ask that scheduled maintenance of the site, which would necessitate cutting off service, be postponed.[9] To some extent, Twitter was useful; a feed established by opposition candidate Mir Hossein Mousavi quickly had 7,000 followers, and the topic aggregator, #Iranelection, was seeing about 30 new posts each minute. The spirit of the Twitter users' efforts was reflected in a Tweet, "One person = one broadcaster."[10]

Twitter was helpful in keeping the world informed about events in Iran, but the spread of information was largely dependent on a relay system that relied on Twitterers outside the country. Sysomos, a Canadian web analytics company, found only 8,600 Twitter users whose profiles indicated that they were based within Iran, and some estimates have been considerably lower.[11] On the ground where the protests were taking place, Farsi websites, text messages, and word-of-mouth contact proved most valuable.[12]

For news organizations and the general public, relying on Twitter should be accompanied by considerable caution. Usually, people sending Tweets are unknown and their accuracy is difficult to gauge. During the Iran protests, Twitterers tended to greatly over-state the numbers of demonstrators, and they also forwarded rumor as "news"—so-and-so had been arrested, the army was planning a coup, a new election would take place, and so on. Journalists covering Iran from afar, as most of them were, found themselves constantly evaluating unverifiable information from sources they did not know. As a general principle of reporting, such information would be discarded unless it was corroborated, but the world's curiosity about events in Iran forced compromises, and Tweeted information, sometimes with disclaimers, found its way into mainstream coverage.

News organizations increasingly use information from citizen journalists to supplement their traditional news gathering, especially on their websites. The *New York Times, Huffington Post,* and CNN were among the news organizations committed to real-time coverage even when that required using unverified material. CNN has a website, iReport.com, dedicated to citizen journalists' work. It tells visitors that "the stories in this section are not edited, fact-checked, or screened before they post. Only the ones marked 'CNN iReport' have been vetted by CNN." Some of these are broadcast on CNN newscasts. During the first two weeks of the 2009 Iran upheaval, CNN received 5,200 Iran-related submissions, of which 180 were approved for use on CNN newscasts.[13]

Social media provide greater heft to criticism of traditional information providers. CNN found itself targeted by Twitterers during the first days of the Iran uprising because of allegedly short-changing coverage of events in Tehran and elsewhere in the country. Tweets marked "#cnnfail" criticized the network, illustrating that those using Twitter recognize that they are merely sources, not replacements, for the large news organizations that can reach mass publics, and so they will be insistent about getting the TV networks and other major players to pick up the topics of their Tweets.[14]

Given the limited number of Twitter users in Iran, it is important to not overrate its impact, particularly as an organizational tool. But, as Jared Keller pointed out, "the Green movement remains the first major world event broadcast worldwide almost entirely via social media. Given the extent of the Iranian regime of repression, the amount of information publicized real-time through social networks allowed the international community an unprecedented peek into the turmoil afflicting Iran. For the Greens, the international reaction to the post-election violence gave the movement critical international visibility."[15] When the BBC, CNN, and other major news organizations cannot be on the scene, citizen journalists may become the outside world's best sources of information.

In addition to Twitter, YouTube was instrumental in drawing the world's attention to events in Iran. Founded in 2005, YouTube is an online video-sharing site. Its existence is due to the pervasiveness of inexpensive video cameras, including those in some mobile phones. Statistics about YouTube use (from YouTube's own website) are staggering: more than 2 billion views per day; 35 hours of video uploaded every minute; more video uploaded to YouTube in 60 days than the three major US television networks created in 60 years.[16]

YouTube can sometimes transcend the questions about veracity that face social media. Some videos on the site are of questionable provenance, but some are obviously real. Videos from Iran that showed the numbers of demonstrators and intensity of the protests brought home to the world the seriousness of the challenge to the Iranian regime. One savage moment had particular resonance worldwide.

Neda

On June 20, 2009, Neda Agha-Soltan (her name would be misspelled many times during the coming days) left her parents' Tehran home to join the protests against Ahmadinejad's victory in the presidential election. Neda was by no means a hard-core radical; she had voted eight days earlier and was furious about the reported results. She met her friend and music teacher Hamid Panahi and they ventured into the chaos of the politically charged streets. They encountered government forces, which were using tear gas against the demonstrators. Neda, Hamid, and two others retreated and drove away in Neda's car, but soon they were caught in a massive traffic jam and so left the car on a side street. They joined other protestors and were soon being chased by antiriot police.

Then, a single gunshot. It was apparently fired by a sniper on a rooftop. Neda said, "I'm burning, I'm burning," and slumped to the ground, bleeding profusely. The bullet had apparently struck her heart; as she lay on the ground blood flowed from her chest, then from her mouth and nose.[17]

Someone nearby used a cell phone to capture video of Neda as she went to the ground and died, less than a minute later. The images are gruesome and gripping; a close-up shows the blood running in streams across her face.

Within moments, the person who filmed the murder had e-mailed the video to several friends, one of whom was in the Netherlands, beyond the barriers the Iranian government had erected to keep people within the country from accessing YouTube. Minutes later, the friend in Holland posted it on YouTube, and shortly thereafter it appeared on CNN. Soon the whole world knew Neda.[18]

Like many other Internet tools, YouTube disseminates information globally and at lightning speed. With millions throughout the world already paying attention to events in Iran, the "viral" spread of the Neda video was no surprise. It appears in numerous versions on YouTube, some of which have been viewed more than a million times.

Most significantly, the video transformed the world's perception of the Iran uprising. Before, for most of the world, it had been a remote event, with anonymous demonstrators protesting something most people outside Iran did not care about. It was just more politics. But now, there was a name and a face; a beautiful young woman dying in full view of millions of people. Even people who knew nothing about the Ahmadinejad regime (or even about Iran) became angry about the murder of Neda.

That sounds simplistic, and it is. But high-speed, global media can transcend conventional political reasoning. Watch Neda's death—the video is still, several years later, available on YouTube—and see how you react. This was a person, not an issue. She was Neda, and YouTube brought her close to millions. Although some argue that video can touch the heart while bypassing the brain, as a matter of practical politics, dramatic images have innate power that cannot be disregarded.

Iranian government officials responded to Neda's murder in their usual heavy-handed way. First, they denied it had happened, then they said it was a CIA plot, then they barred the public from Neda's funeral and prohibited her family from hanging a black mourning banner, then they posted soldiers to keep the public away from Neda's unmarked grave, and then they went back to denying any responsibility.

They convinced no one.

Iran's Countermeasures

Although questions remain about the precise effects of online tools during the Iran uprising, the Iranian government recognized that these tools were helping protestors to challenge the regime's brute force. The ability of protestors to communicate freely with the world and to disseminate material such as the Neda video was viewed by officials as a serious threat that could emerge again. It could not be allowed to continue.

The way to fix this for the long term is this: cut off most of Iran from the global Internet and allow access instead to just an Iran-only Intranet that would be closely supervised by the government. This would be a big task; Internet World Stats estimated in 2011 that about 33 million Iranians—43 percent of the population—were online (up from 30 percent two years earlier).[19] But the Iranian leadership apparently believes it is worth the effort. As the *Wall Street Journal* reported in May 2011, Iranian officials fear not only active communication among antigovernment activists, but also the influx of Western ideas and culture that stream through cyberspace and onto Iranians' computers. Ayatollah Khamenei and others have called this "soft war." In a November 2009 speech to the Basij paramilitary organization, Khamenei said, "In a soft war the enemy tries to make use of advanced and cultural and communication tools to spread lies and rumors."

At least at the outset, the regime would pay attention to the demands of international commerce. Banks, large companies, and government ministries would still have access to the regular global Internet. Most Iranians, however, would use a national network that would, said one official, be "aimed at Muslims on an ethical and moral level."

The powerful Revolutionary Guard is at the forefront of the new communication order in Iran. In late 2009, it acquired a majority stake in the state telecom agency, giving the Guard control of all of Iran's communication networks. The Guard has also reportedly created a "cyber army" with a goal of training 250,000 computer hackers who would be put to work as directed by the government.[20]

Will this effort work? Perhaps for a while, if the regime throws enough resources into the venture. But technology wizards around the world have proved adept at staying a step ahead of governments, or at least catching up quickly when the need arises, although some governments have become more adept at keeping the upper hand.

The choke-points that the Iranian leadership assumes it can use to cut off their country from the rest of the online world might be bypassed within a short time, and then the Iranian government would need to find additional obstacles to put in place. This is how the "soft war" is likely to be fought.

The High-Tech Contest

Iran's is not the only government trying to protect itself from what it sees as hostile cyber incursions. Democratic and nondemocratic states, especially their security agencies, monitor new technologies as they appear, looking for ways to penetrate secret (or perhaps just private) communication.

In Uganda, shortly before elections there in early 2011, the state-run Uganda Communications Commission ordered the country's telephone companies to intercept text messages containing the words "Egypt," "Mubarak," "people power," "dictator," "teargas," and others.[21] The Ugandan leadership apparently feared a copycat uprising and did not want online models to be available to those who might want to organize such an effort.

In Egypt, the Mubarak government, during its final throes, ordered Vodafone to distribute text messages appealing to "honest and loyal men to confront the traitors and criminals and protect our people and honor." Other messages urged attendance at pro-Mubarak rallies. The messages were signed "Vodafone" and "Egypt Lovers." Vodafone issued a statement protesting the government's demands, saying, "We have made clear that all messages should be transparent and clearly attributable to the originator." Vodafone also said that its competitors had been compelled to send similar messages.[22]

Such activities have been referred to as "Repression 2.0." Pro-government messages appeared on the Facebook pages and Twitter accounts of Syrian political activists in May 2011, during antiregime protests there.[23]

Skype, the Internet telephone service created in 2003, has drawn special attention from intelligence services because calls are encrypted. Skype had 663 million registered users by the end of 2009 and had won 13 percent of the international calling market by 2010.[24]

During the Mubarak years, Egypt's secret police believed that Skype posed a threat because, as was stated in an internal memo, it was "a safe and encrypted Internet communication system to which most extremist groups have resorted to communicate with each other." The Egyptian authorities purchased software that would intercept the audio through the user's computer before it was encrypted. This "spyware" was spread and implanted like a computer virus, and it worked. After the Egyptian revolution, antigovernment activists found police files with details of their Skype conversations.

Elsewhere, the Chinese government, as in many cases, is ahead of the game, requiring Skype, before being allowed to enter the Chinese market, to employ filters that block politically sensitive words that turn up in users' text chats.[25] Even in democratic countries, Skype-hacking and other monitoring of new media will continue to pose legal and ethical questions as governments and publics decide how much intrusion into communication is acceptable. It is safe to assume that intelligence agencies throughout the world are considering ways to tamper not only with technology, but also with content. Twitter, Facebook, YouTube, and other venues are ripe for manipulation through planting of information twisted for political reasons. Given how easily that can be done by an individual intent on making mischief, consider the damage that could be caused by a sophisticated intelligence operation.

A notable instance of fraudulent online identity was the case of the blogger "Gay Girl in Damascus," who turned out to be a male American living in Scotland. The "Gay Girl" blogs described protests in Syria as well as the life of a young, gay woman named Amina. Amina's blogs about her exploits had been reported by major Western news organizations. When the purported cousin of the blogger reported in early June 2011 that Amina had been kidnapped, presumably by the Syrian police, Internet campaigns demanded her release. No one had ever met Amina face-to-face, and skeptics raised questions about her existence. Finally, Tom McMaster, an American studying at the University of Edinburgh, came forward and admitted that he had written the blogs. He said he had done so to spread the story about the antigovernment protests in Syria, but his efforts ended up giving credence to the Assad regime's claims that outsiders were interfering in Syrian affairs.[26]

This case underscores the ease with which online fraud can be perpetrated. A dangerous naïveté pervades the treatment of material that appears in social media or other online content. Even many news organizations set aside the skepticism that is essential to journalism when they come upon compelling stories online. The possibility that something is "too good to be true" should be taken seriously, and if corroboration is not feasible, news organizations should not disseminate the story. For the individual information consumer, without the skill or resources to confirm veracity, resisting manipulation is more difficult, but as "media literacy" becomes more sophisticated, standards may rise and fraud may become less common.

This is yet another cautionary note about the media tools that have been embraced so enthusiastically in some quarters. They are beneficial in many ways, but they are also vulnerable in many ways.

Keeping Information Channels Open

With varied degrees of success, Iran, Egypt, Syria, and other countries choked off Internet access within their countries. Efforts to avoid such censorship have spawned a mini-industry that builds ways to evade governments' electronic blockades. Funding for these projects may come from NGOs and from governments that want to keep information flowing. Design of these measures is in the hands of techies who may work for intelligence agencies or on their own. The reasons of those who do this work may be idealistic, but particularly in the cases of government-backed innovation, diplomatic and security interests are usually at the heart of the ventures. Speaking of the efforts of reformers, US secretary of state Hillary Clinton said: "There is a historic opportunity to effect positive change, change America supports. So we're focused on helping them do that, on helping them talk to each other, to their communities, to their governments, and to the world."[27]

As of mid-2011, the concept receiving considerable attention was "Internet in a suitcase," which relies on equipment small enough to be smuggled into a country, if necessary. It would be used to set up a "mesh network" or "Intermesh" that would be a small-scale wireless Internet. Another version of an alternative network relies on Bluetooth technology (best known in the West for its wireless headsets) to send information from one mobile telephone to others.[28]

Such efforts reflect recognition of the Internet and mobile phones as valued tools in campaigns for political change. No longer are these just toys for rich nations, and no longer are they wholly subject to control by governments that fear open communication. As access to these technological assets continues to increase, the openness of networks will become more important and efforts to ensure that openness will become more contentious.

Something Other Than Diplomacy

Consider the role of the president of the United States when the Iran uprising of 2009 began. What should he have done? He could have strongly endorsed the protestors and even held out the promise of US assistance if there was regime change. That would have shown the United States to be a forceful champion of liberty and might have encouraged those who were intent on toppling Ahmadinejad. A presidential address along these lines would have sent a powerful message to the world. It would have been good theater.

It also would have played into the hands of Ahmadinejad, who was searching for a way to attribute the protests to a US-engineered plot. The good theater might have produced political benefits in the West, but they would have been short-lived and the diplomatic damage would have been substantial. Iranians who counted on US assistance could well have ended up dead, victims of the regime's security forces.

So political leaders must get out on the tightrope and try to maintain their balance. Here is what President Obama said in his opening remarks at a June 23, 2009, news conference: "I've made it clear that the United States respects the sovereignty of the Islamic Republic of Iran, and is not interfering with Iran's affairs. But we must also bear witness to the courage and the dignity of the Iranian people, and to a remarkable opening within Iranian society. And we deplore the violence against innocent civilians anywhere that it takes place. The Iranian people are trying to have a debate about their future. Some in Iran—some in the Iranian government, in particular—are trying to avoid that debate by accusing the United States and others in the West of instigating protests over the election. These accusations are patently false. They're an obvious attempt to distract people from what is truly taking place within Iran's borders. This tired strategy of using old tensions to scapegoat other countries won't work anymore in Iran. This is not about the United States or the West; this is about the people of Iran, and the future that they—and only they—will choose. The Iranian people can speak for themselves."[29]

One reporter at the news conference cited a Republican US senator who had called Obama's response to events in Iran "timid and weak." When asked by another reporter "what took so long" for the president to use strong language, Obama replied: "As soon as violence broke out—in fact, in anticipation of potential violence—we were very clear in saying that violence was unacceptable, that that was not how governments operate with respect to their people. My role has been to say the United States is not going to be a foil for the Iranian government to try to blame what's happening on the streets of Tehran on the CIA or on the White House, that this is an issue that is led by and given voice to the frustrations of the Iranian people."[30]

This case illustrates the difficult path world leaders must follow as they try to protect their foreign relations strategy from being shredded by time-related pressures. A constructive disconnect exists—and should exist—between the rate at which information flows to the public, including images such as those of Neda's death, and policymakers' responses. This process is complicated by the public political pressure that can be engendered by conventional news coverage and, increasingly, by social media content.

To respond otherwise than Obama did in the Iran case would have been something other than diplomacy—more posturing than policy. But the pressure to be quick rather than smart continues to grow, particularly as greater synergy develops between new and traditional media forums. Major television networks, for example, increasingly take cues about the news agenda, as well as specific content, from social media sources. From a "the more news, the better" standpoint, this is fine, but along with questions about corroboration and general journalistic quality, this approach carries with it a threat of intellectual incoherence. The public receives so much information that only the most dramatic matters stand out, while context is ignored. Such dramatic fare can produce a visceral reaction that may quickly lead to "Do something!" political pressure.

This is the environment in which policymakers now must work. Not being swept along by the information deluge requires considerable resolve.

WikiLeaks and the
Appeal of Transparency

During 2010, WikiLeaks, a nonprofit organization that publishes secret government information, released material about the Afghanistan War, the Iraq War, and US State Department diplomatic cables. The organization's sources had found ways to tap into the US government's online repositories of internal documents. The diplomatic material included cables from US embassies that featured frank assessments of foreign leaders and policies. Some of these alleged high-level corruption in foreign governments, and others included instructions from the State Department about intelligence-gathering tasks for diplomatic personnel. Initial conduits for this information included the *New York Times,* the *Guardian, El Pais, Le Monde,* and *Der Spiegel,* and their reports were quickly picked up by other news organizations around the world.

The US government expressed suitable anguish, defending secrecy while endorsing transparency. White House press secretary Robert Gibbs issued a statement on the eve of publication of the leaks. It said: "By its very nature, field reporting to Washington is candid and often incomplete information. It is not an expression of policy, nor does it always shape final policy decisions. Nevertheless, these cables could compromise private discussions with foreign governments and opposition leaders, and when the substance of private conversations is printed on the front pages of newspapers across the world, it can deeply impact not only US foreign policy interests, but those of our allies and friends around the world."[31] In response to a reporter's question the following day, Gibbs said: "Open and transparent government is something that the President believes is truly important. But the stealing of classified information and its dissemination is a crime."[32]

Secretary of State Hillary Rodham Clinton condemned the leaks: "This disclosure is not just an attack on America's foreign policy interests. It is an attack on the international community—the alliances and partnerships, the conversations and negotiations, that safeguard global security and advance economic prosperity.... Every country, including the United States, must be able to have candid conversations about the people and nations with whom they deal. And every country, including the United States, must be able to have honest, private dialogue with other countries about issues of common concern.... We count on the space of trust that confidentiality provides."[33]

Like the cushion of time that diplomats once relied upon, the "space of trust" afforded by confidentiality has become a victim of media technologies that are appealing because of their speed and accessibility. Those characteristics do not come without a price, as policymakers continue to learn. Transparency is in many ways an important democratic value, but a case can be made that it should have limits. The public should be informed about the contents of a treaty that its country has entered into, but that does not mean that the negotiating process—with its give-and-take and trial balloons—should be open to general scrutiny.[34] The spotlight that allows transparency can be inhibiting. Negotiating may give way to posturing, and the good faith that is essential to productive diplomacy will become increasingly scarce.

Favors governments do for one another may also be less likely to be granted. In counterterrorism, the risk of exposure might make cooperation between countries' intelligence agencies seem too politically risky. For cautious policymakers, every electronic conversation that was once thought to be private must now be expected to become public. That means many such conversations will no longer take place, or if they do they will have little value. Confidential sources will no longer come forward if they think their identities might leak out. Overall, information could be much harder to come by.

From the public's standpoint, WikiLeaks can be viewed in several ways. It can seen as an evil enterprise undermining the government's essential functions, or it can be applauded as a way to let the public know more about what its government is doing, which is especially valuable when the government has not been forthcoming or honest. Debate about these matters, which is part of a larger consideration of transparency, will continue.

Governments' responses to WikiLeaks have ranged from planning legal action against the leakers to considering how to deal with the vulnerabilities of cyber communication. Some have suggested going back to messages on paper (perhaps sent via carrier pigeon?), or relying on telephone calls on more secure systems. These have good-old-days appeal, but both paper and phone calls can be intercepted as easily as can Internet transmissions.

However security might be enhanced, diplomats must recognize that even the newest versions of communication are unlikely to be totally secure. A whole generation of hackers will, for a variety of purposes, seek—and most probably find—ways to penetrate what had been thought to be private diplomatic dispatches. Openness will be forced upon the diplomatic process, requiring changes in the way business is done and perhaps also making hypocrisy less affordable. Disingenuous public praise for corrupt foreign officials might become less frequent if diplomats know that frank evaluations of that corruption could become public.

Diplomatic cables are likely to become less interesting, with controversial matters stripped out. This will make them less valuable to decision makers. Participants in policy debates will be more wary and less forthcoming, yet another blow to the intellectual value of such long-distance discussions.

The WikiLeaks controversy is another milepost in the evolutionary journey of diplomacy. As dependence on technology has grown, the speed of the diplomatic process has accelerated, which poses many challenges. As the same time, the notion that diplomacy is something existing outside the public domain has become largely obsolete. The public is no longer a distant stakeholder but instead is able, on increasingly frequent occasions, to look over the diplomat's shoulder and pass judgment on what is seen.

Speed and transparency are defining today's high-tech world. Not everyone likes that, but clinging to the past is not feasible. Diplomats who yearn for the good old days will be left behind, while others work at devising new kinds of diplomacy.

★　★　★

At the heart of the changes in the conduct of foreign policy is not technology per se, but rather the expanded role of a public that can gather more information from more sources than ever before. This means that the public expects to be informed and diplomats, regardless of whether they like the idea, must bring the public into their work.

Such a change involves a substantive conceptual readjustment of how diplomacy is envisioned. The "striped-pants set" has been gone from the scene for quite a while now, and today's diplomats are coming to understand that their constituency is larger than solely their professional colleagues.

Because of the wide array of easily accessible communication tools, people know more and expect more. The notion that diplomats can do most of their business outside the public's view is anachronistic, and it does not matter that some diplomats can make a good case for the value of secrecy in negotiations and other aspects of their work. Media phenomena such as Twitter feeds, YouTube postings, and WikiLeaks-type revelations make secrecy problematic on many levels.

Needed today are new kinds of diplomacy and new kinds of diplomats. National interests will still be championed, and skill in dealing with other states will still be essential. Performance, however, will be measured not only in meeting rooms of foreign ministries, but also on computer monitors and mobile telephone screens. Any nation that allows its diplomatic establishment to lag behind will be hurting only itself.

CHAPTER 5

THE EXPEDITIONARY DIPLOMAT AND THE CASE FOR PUBLIC DIPLOMACY

In his 1939 classic, *Diplomacy*, Sir Harold Nicolson wrote, "In the days of the old diplomacy it would have been regarded as an act of unthinkable vulgarity to appeal to the common people upon any issue of international policy." Nicolson lamented technological advances such as "the invention of the wireless," which gave "a vast impetus to propaganda as a method of policy" and allowed manipulators such as Adolf Hitler to wield "a formidable weapon of popular excitement."[1]

Today, it would be an act of unthinkable stupidity to disregard "the common people" (more felicitously referred to as "the public") in the conduct of foreign affairs. Propaganda can still be effective, but the public is not at such a disadvantage as it once was because of the vast array of information providers that can offset, as well as deliver, the messages of propagandists. Empowered by their unprecedented access to information, many people have a better sense of how they fit into the global community, and they are less inclined to entrust diplomacy solely to diplomats. They want to be part of the process.

With members of the public having rising expectations about participating in democratic diplomacy, their activism affects not only policymakers of their own country, but also those who implement the foreign policy of other states. This expectation makes the diplomat play more of a conventional political role than she or he may have done in the past, with a constituency far larger than the traditional foreign policy establishment. Shrewd domestic politicians, such as George H. W. Bush's secretary of state James A. Baker and Hillary Rodham Clinton, secretary of state during Barack Obama's presidency, possess skills that have become essential supplements to the traditional art of diplomacy. They recognize that their domestic public is affected by the 24-hour news cycle, as are publics in many of the countries with which they deal, and so their diplomacy must reflect sensitivity to shifting political currents, at home and abroad. Thanks to recent communication tools—from satellite television to Twitter—the world intrudes into more lives than ever before.

A reordering of relationships is underway among those who make policy, those who carry it out, and those who are affected by it. Henry Kissinger observed in a 2011 interview that "new technologies make it much easier to acquire factual knowledge, though they make it harder in a way to process it because one is flooded with information, but what one needs for diplomacy is to develop a concept of what one is trying to achieve. The Internet drives you to the immediate resolution of symptoms but may make it harder to get to the essence of the problems. It's easier to know what people are saying, but the question is whether diplomats have time to connect that with its deeper historical context."[2]

Balancing recognition of historical context with the pressures generated by new information and communication technologies will require a new approach to the construction of diplomacy and to being a diplomat.

The Expeditionary Diplomat

Marc Grossman, former US under secretary of state and, as of this writing, the special envoy to Afghanistan and Pakistan, has suggested that the State Department create "a new personnel specialty: the 'expeditionary diplomat,'" who would serve "in the hardest places at a moment's notice," working primarily on postconflict reconstruction and stabilization projects. Some of these diplomats' in-the-field skills would be acquired through training provided by the Department of Defense and the Central Intelligence Agency.[3]

To expand on Grossman's idea, this would be part of a redefinition of diplomatic service that would enlarge the diplomat's realm to include much more direct contact with the public in the country in which she or he serves. (Many diplomats already spend considerable time working outside their embassy's walls, but others remain reluctant to extend their engagement with the host country beyond diplomat-to-diplomat contacts.)

This would be a significant shift, moving public diplomacy into a more central role in a nation's foreign policy, and putting greater emphasis on government-to-people rather than government-to-government relationships. It also would involve a substantive change in the diplomat's mission, as she or he might sometimes be a direct service provider. For example, rather than just talking about a country's need for a better supply of clean water, the expeditionary diplomat would be involved in creating and supervising projects that provided that water, with emphasis on working directly with the public—rather than just the government—of the host nation.

Granted, this might often prove easier in principle than in practice. Some host countries would consider such an effort to be meddling in their domestic affairs and would not allow it. But just as the domestic politics of numerous countries are being changed by information and communication technologies, so too are relationships between countries. Traditional concepts governing diplomatic practice can be updated or they can become obsolete. This choice should be contemplated carefully by policymakers.

If diplomats are to expand their roles, social media will be helpful, and as soon as penetration of technology expands, essential. As members of the public increase their use of these tools, they will expect to find policy-related material through them, much as they have come to expect government leaders to remain in touch with the public through television and radio, and now through websites and, increasingly, their own Twitter feeds and other social media connections. (The US State Department has created its own "Social Media Hub" to assist American diplomats in using social media tools by offering practical guidance and showcasing best practices.)

Using these newer media requires appreciation of what they can and cannot do. Media theorist Brian Solis observed: "One of the greatest lessons in social media is that everything begins with listening....Not only are new media channels rich with insight, they are also interactive. There are people on the other side who have expectations of recognition, acknowledgement, and engagement."[4] Listening is also the foundation of public diplomacy; it is the best way to learn about the public with which you are trying to connect.

The interactive nature of social media underscores the importance of listening because the time is long past when one-way pronouncements rather than balanced conversation could suffice.

The need to listen is related to what some governments now consider a fundamental human right—the right to free expression. That concept is not new, but it is now much more than a theoretical ideal because social media and related communication technologies make it feasible in practice. The events of 2011 in the Arab world well illustrate the widespread eagerness with which this right has been embraced and the effect it has on the relationship between those who govern and those who are governed, and with those communicating from outside, including diplomats.

As free expression takes hold among larger constituencies, policymakers are coming to understand that they must respond by explaining—and sometimes defending—their issues positions. US under secretary of state Judith McHale noted that "in the world of social media, if you don't provide a context for what you're doing, other people will interpret your actions for you....We produce 100 foreign language Twitter feeds. That's the character of 21st century diplomacy."[5]

Although hearing and responding to foreign publics is crucial, none of this means that social media can be just casually used to bolster foreign policy. In an official environment, tools such as blogs might be *too* egalitarian, appearing to level the policymaking playing field when, in reality, hierarchies are very much still in place. Creating and implementing foreign policy is only partly a democratic process, and communication practices that seem to indicate otherwise can be unhelpful. At some point, opening the diplomatic process can move from orderly participation to a more anarchic situation. Policymakers are feeling their way along as they try to determine what the appropriate levels of organizational openness might be. US State Department official Duncan MacInnes said, "Because blogging tends to be a very informal, chatty way of working, it is actually very dangerous to blog."[6]

A critical element of real-time diplomacy will be determining how the "very dangerous" social media that encourage individual expression can be constructively incorporated within the policymaking process. For expeditionary diplomats to be successful, they will need latitude in their operations as they work with publics that possess new-found sophistication in the arts of communication. Senior policymakers in Washington and other capitals should recognize this and develop new training and operational guidelines so their expeditionary diplomats may serve as the principal implementers of their countries' public diplomacy.

In Syria during 2011, US ambassador Robert Ford courageously and forcefully made certain that US diplomatic efforts would not vanish during the Assad regime's repression of public protests. Using Facebook and other methods, Ford kept up a running conversation with the Syrian public, explaining US policy, debunking myths, and (simply) maintaining a presence. Ford said of this: "My whole purpose in being in Syria is to be able to communicate not only with the Syrian government but with the Syrian people more generally....The Syrian television operated by the state, operated by the dictatorship, is not credible and tells all kinds of lies. So we are looking for ways to reach out to the Syrian public through social media, through things like Facebook, and by going out and about in the country....It's important to bear witness to what the Syrian government is doing."[7]

That is the kind of assertive diplomacy that will be essential in a fast-moving, contentious world.

The Rise of Public Diplomacy

Public diplomacy recognizes the importance in foreign affairs of reaching out directly to publics, not just other states' officialdom. The outreach is most often undertaken by governments, but international organizations, NGOs, corporations, and other entities may develop their own public diplomacy efforts. For purposes of this discussion, the focus will be on governments' work in this field.

The first great American public diplomat was Benjamin Franklin, dispatched to France to bolster support for the American colonies' movement toward independence from Great Britain. With flare and shrewdness, Franklin cultivated the French, who later provided indispensible aid during the American Revolution.

More recently, highpoints of American public diplomacy have included the Peace Corps, begun in 1961 during John F. Kennedy's presidency. Kennedy aide Theodore Sorensen wrote that the Peace Corps showed "the American spirit of generosity through face-to-face contacts and practical assistance, building goodwill not through a bureaucracy, propaganda, wealthy tourists, or American business-men, but through friendly, courteous, helpful Americans from all walks of life interacting daily with ordinary locals." In addition to its foreign policy value, added Sorensen, the program "helped make young Americans feel reconnected to the national interest."[8] The founding director of the Peace Corps, R. Sargent Shriver, said that serving in the Peace Corps was an "unparalleled opportunity to win friends and advance the cause of peace and freedom."[9]

Despite the many ways in which the Peace Corps has been suc-cessful, questions have been raised about whether it remains a cost-efficient way to serve US interests. Charles Kenny has pointed out that "the Peace Corps is operating in a world where people in even remote regions have exponentially greater access to sources of information about American culture and foreign policy than they had in 1961." Also, notes Kenny, the Peace Corps is more costly than other efforts, such as the Fulbright Program that sup-ports exchanges of scholars between the United States and other countries.[10]

Kenny's argument may have merit, but so does having Peace Corps volunteers on the ground, serving in ways similar to what Grossman envisions for expeditionary diplomats. Kenny correctly points out knowledge about America is far greater today than it was a half-century ago, but the information available today about the United States comes from diverse sources and a considerable amount of it is unfavorable, and some of that is also false. As a matter of national self-interest, having diplomats, Peace Corps vol-unteers, or other representatives physically present is important, whether to complement or counterbalance the electronic surge of information.

A more recent but exceptionally useful public diplomacy effort is the President's Emergency Plan for AIDS Relief (PEPFAR), which was enacted in 2003 during George W. Bush's first term and was designed to provide antiviral treatment to 2 million HIV-infected persons, to prevent 7 million new infections, and to support care for 10 million people fighting the disease.[11] As with the Peace Corps, this program directly touches people's lives, providing substantive evidence of America as a valuable friend. Funding for PEPFAR has been renewed and the program's mission expanded.

Such projects also serve the national interest of the sponsoring country. US health and human services secretary Tommy G. Thompson observed that "health diplomacy recognizes that the health and security of our own citizens is tied directly to that of our neighbors around the world. Through the bond of health care, this strategy builds strong, lasting relationships—relationships that secure our nation's future and build a strong, stable global community." Thompson added that health-related aid could help prevent conflict: "The link between political unrest and poor health is well established. Studies show that nations with the highest mortality rates for infants and children under age five are most likely to engage in war."[12]

These programs require the approval of the governments of the countries in which they operate, but they are designed to directly touch the lives of individuals. More generally, public diplomacy includes cultural and educational exchanges and other projects that rarely merit international headlines but can be exceptionally effective in shaping public views of a particular country. Peace Corps volunteers digging a well for a South American village, and a physician funded by PEPFAR treating an HIV-positive pregnant woman in Africa are examples of ways to quietly shape public attitudes about the United States.

On a grander scale, international broadcasting by the Voice of America and other entities can be effective—as it was during the cold war—depending on the course of events and the targeted public's hunger for information. The BBC, China's CCTV, Germany's Deutsche Welle, Qatar's Al Jazeera (discussed later in this chapter), and other state-funded broadcasters are the still useful antecedents of newer media tools.

Public diplomacy can also be advanced by traditional rhetoric. It was at the heart of President Barack Obama's speech in Cairo in June 2009, in which he said: "I've come here to Cairo to seek a new beginning between the United States and Muslims around the world, one based on mutual interest and mutual respect, and one based upon the truth that America and Islam are not exclusive and need not be in competition. Instead, they overlap, and share common principles—principles of justice and progress; tolerance and the dignity of all human beings."[13]

Note that he spoke to "Muslims around the world"; there is little mention of nations, other than the United States, in the speech. He was trying to connect with individuals, knowing that there was great variation in the level of affection citizens in Muslim countries held for their governments. The speech also reflected Obama's understanding that while relations with these governments (such as Egypt's Mubarak regime) were manageable in a *realpolitik* sense, winning the support of publics was a far more difficult task. He presumably did not foresee that these publics would assert themselves as forcefully as they did just two years later, but he did know that the interests of the United States required constituency building within the Muslim world through public diplomacy in addition to conventional government-to-government ties.

Public diplomacy, like other elements of real-time diplomacy, is directly related to media accessibility and influence. Exponents of democracy endorse and take advantage of the reduction of barriers to information and the involvement of global publics in international affairs. But when Harold Nicolson voiced his concern about "the common people," he was not sounding merely an elitist alarm. He was warning, quite wisely, about the manipulative power of propaganda (which skeptics might argue is little different from public diplomacy). "Propaganda" is defined by some as being self-serving to the point of being untruthful. That definition is debatable, but the pejorative connotation lingers. Those conducting public diplomacy should recognize this and find ways to ensure that their efforts do not—in fact as well as in perception—stray from the truth.

Some historical and comparative examples may be useful.

Hitler's Lies

Proponents of public diplomacy are not eager to point to Nazi Germany as a practitioner of their field, but Adolf Hitler's regime recognized the need to reach out to foreign publics as part of its strategy to buy time while building its strength and to undermine alliances that would be hostile to Germany.

Hitler himself learned early in his career that demagoguery and lies could serve him well in his climb to power. In *Mein Kampf,* published in 1925, he wrote: "The art of propaganda consists precisely in being able to awaken the imagination of the public through an appeal to their feelings, in finding the appropriate psychological form that will arrest the attention and appeal to the hearts of the national masses."[14] When Hitler became chancellor of Germany in 1933, he appointed Joseph Goebbels as minister of public enlightenment and propaganda. In their propaganda campaigns, the Nazis stressed the threats of external enemies who had imposed the Treaty of Versailles on Germany, and internal enemies, principally Jews and Communists. For a nation looking for vengeance and scapegoats, this propaganda proved effective.

The Nazis also reached out to foreign publics, trying to convince them that Germany was not a threat to them and that their countries should not go to war with Germany. In these efforts, the Nazis adapted their propaganda machinery to requirements of public diplomacy—sometimes trying to drive a wedge between a foreign public and its government, sometimes attempting to be softly lulling. The Germans made heavy use of radio programs aimed directly at British and American listeners. Beginning with his broadcasts from Germany in April 1939, New York–born William Joyce, known more widely as Lord Haw-Haw, told British listeners every night that their government was corrupt and exploitive, representing only the upper classes that cared little for the needs of the mass public. American broadcaster Edward R. Murrow noted that "each time he creates a doubt in the mind of a listener, he wins a victory. The British began by ridiculing him and are now taking him a little more seriously."[15]

When the German blitzkrieg began in the spring of 1940, Joyce switched from preaching about social injustice in Britain to warning about military disaster awaiting the Allies. He told his listeners: "England is ripe for invasion....You might as well expect help from an army of mastodons as from the United States....Either England gives in before it is too late, or she will be beaten." He criticized Winston Churchill, saying: "Perhaps if the British people could speak, they would ask for peace. But since the official voice of England asks not for peace but for destruction, it is destruction we must provide."[16]

As Britain made ready to fight for its life, Lord Haw-Haw's appeal evaporated and his substantial British audience tuned him out. Joyce tried to recapture his listeners by targeting America: "It stands to reason that the White House and Wall Street have only one fundamental interest in the rest of the struggle; namely, to induce the British to prolong it until Britain herself is so weakened that her possessions in the Western Hemisphere, including her capital invest-ments, fall into American hands." With Germany on the attack, however, Joyce's speculation about US intentions did not win back his listeners.[17]

Meanwhile, Americans were also hearing from the Germans. A German radio service for North America had been started in 1933, and as Hitler embarked on his course toward war the broad-casts praised isolationism, criticized Britain, and portrayed the new Germany in the best light, claiming, for example, that Hitler was simply trying "to straighten out some of the political and economic confusion with which Central and Eastern Europe were plagued."[18] Once the war began in 1939, this radio service sent America more than 11 hours of programming each day, including 9 news programs and 5 commentaries. Among the broadcasters was Iowa native Fred Kaltenbach, who each week delivered an "open letter" that began, "Dear Harry and the folks back home in Iowa." In one of these letters, he warned his listeners about British propaganda: "The American people are to be led to believe that England and France are the last hopes of democracy, and that Germany is seeking to beat them only because they are democratic. Stuff and nonsense!" On another occasion, Kaltenbach said, "Let it be said, once and for all, a German victory in this war is no threat to democracy—and certainly not to American democracy."[19] The broadcasts attempted to justify German policy by comparing the seizure of the Polish Corridor with the US annexation of Texas, and likened Hitler's con-cept of *Lebensraum*—ensuring "living space" by controlling Central Europe—to the Monroe Doctrine.[20]

In their appeals to Americans, the task for the Germans was not so much to win support as to help sustain isolationism. In one German newscast, the announcer said, "Above all, we cannot help congratulating the American people on their steadfast, neutral atti-tude...America *is* neutral....She wants to stay neutral."[21]

When American public opinion showed signs of shifting toward a stronger anti-Nazi outlook, the German broadcasts became more pointed. News-related skits tried anti-Semitic appeals, using as their negative characters "Mr. Finkelstein" and "Mr. Rosenbloom." In his broadcasts, Kaltenbach complained about Americans being influ-enced by anti-German propaganda. "The German government and the German people," he said, "have left nothing undone to court

American favor. And how has this been rewarded? With reproaches and rebuffs.... It is not too late, however, to extend the hand of friendship to the strongest power in Europe."[22]

American self-interest was stressed frequently in the German broadcasts, and German–Americans were warned about being victimized by the spreading anti-German feeling: "Don't let it get you down, you German-Americans.... People whose opinions really count will admire you for sticking up for Germany in a fight which is no concern of the United States." Once France was out of the war, the German theme became more stridently anti-British: "England is standing on her last legs. She stands all alone in Europe and there is nothing the United States can do to stave off her defeat at the hands of Germany. And why should she want to? What has England ever done for America?" Similarly, "The fight for a lost cause may be thoroughly honorable in itself," but "it hardly behooves a young, vigorous nation like the United States to stand in the way of progress and the New Order."[23] One of the German commentators argued that "there is a far greater similarity between American democracy and German National Socialism than there is between old-fashioned English class distinction and Americanism."[24]

On any given day in early 1941, the American audience for the German broadcasts was estimated at about 150,000, but there is no evidence that the German radio efforts accomplished anything beyond feeding the gospel according to Goebbels to the small number of Nazi sympathizers in America.[25] If the Nazis' programs created any drag on the pro-British drift in American opinion, it didn't amount to much.

The German radio campaigns directed at Britain and America were, however, an interesting example of the use of broadcasting as an intellectual weapon. Murrow understood what propaganda was designed to do. "The real objective of broadcasting into enemy countries," he said in a report from London, "is to hack away at civilian morale, undermine the will to fight, create doubts as to the honesty and integrity of national leaders, emphasize and exaggerate social and economic inequalities, boast of your own achievements while pointing out that the enemy is without hope and fights for an unworthy cause."[26]

Discussions about public diplomacy rarely touch on these German efforts, partly because they were permeated with evil and partly because they were unsuccessful. They failed because the Nazi lies became so obvious and because Britain's own public diplomacy was far more sophisticated. Winston Churchill had a true ally in Franklin Roosevelt, who was intent on nudging American public opinion toward the point at which helping the British became politically feasible, and Britain had its own campaign to help that process. Churchill embraced "public diplomacy by proxy," using American voices—principally those of journalists such as Murrow—to convince the US public that it was in America's best interest to come to Britain's aid. Murrow's real-time reporting from London's rooftops as the city was bombed by the Germans was an important part of this.[27]

Nazi public diplomacy was largely an exercise in self-justification and fabrication. Much of the German public may have been pliable enough to accept Hitler's message, but most of the rest of the world soon recognized that the Nazis' propaganda had no relation to the truth and should be ignored. Although the Germans used radio as their tool, it was this same medium that undermined their efforts. Reports from Murrow and other American correspondents had far more credibility among US listeners than did foreign voices, even those with American accents. Wanting to hear news from "your own" remains an important factor in information delivery today.

Qatar, Al Jazeera, and the Diplomacy of Influence

The creation of Al Jazeera in 1996 was not just a journalistic venture. It was also creative public diplomacy on the part of the emir of Qatar, Hamad bin Khalifa Al Thani. He wanted to make his tiny, but enormously wealthy, country an international player in matters beyond oil and natural gas production. In the eyes of much of the world, the dominant Arab nations were Egypt—big but poor—and Saudi Arabia—rich but paranoid—and so the emir rightly judged that there was an opening for an opportunistic, media-savvy state to assert itself.

And so, Al Jazeera. Arab audiences were accustomed to getting their television news either from outsiders, such as the BBC or CNN, or from stodgy, state-run channels that steadfastly avoided any topic that might be considered controversial. Al Jazeera brought

Arab audiences news about them presented by voices like theirs. Al Jazeera provided news intended for an entire region, and so its broadcasts made the provincialism enforced by borders less significant.

With the Intifada of 2000 and the US invasion of Afghanistan in 2001, Al Jazeera established itself in the region and around the world as a significant Arab voice. In 2006, Al Jazeera inaugurated its English-language channel, and the network will soon offer Al Jazeera Turkish and Al Jazeera Swahili, making it an even more important global information provider and political player.

Al Jazeera plays a major role in real-time diplomacy. As had been the case with CNN (founded in 1980), policymakers and a sizable number of general viewers pay close attention to a channel offering continuous coverage of important events. Al Jazeera's reporting about Israel's attacks on Gaza in 2008–2009 spurred street demonstrations in Arab countries and put political pressure on Arab governments to do more for the Palestinians. Its continuous live coverage of the Arab revolutions of 2011 was watched throughout the region and around the world, influencing public opinion and governments' responses to events on the ground. Through it all, Qatar was rising in international importance, serving as the site for peace talks about regional conflicts, hosting conferences and debates about the global economy and other topics, and submitting the winning bid to host the 2022 World Cup.

In 2011, Qatar became a principal backer of anti-Qaddafi rebels in Libya, providing financial, humanitarian, and military aid. Al Jazeera was granted exclusive frontline reporting access and rebel leaders issued many of their public statements through the channel. Qatar also helped the rebels establish their own television station. Funding for the channel came primarily from a wealthy Libyan expatriate, while Qatar made available the facilities and technical staff of one of its local channels. Qatar also offered to buy and export oil produced in rebel-held Libyan territory, providing a revenue stream for the insurgents. In the longer term, Qatar expected to play a significant role in managing Libya's oil and gas concessions if the rebels prevailed. The Emir was also winning the gratitude of the NATO nations involved in the military campaign against Qaddafi, and was building his credentials as an Arab Spring supporter without engaging in reforms at home.[28] (It should be noted that Qatar had previously been supportive of the Qaddafi regime, joining in a combined investment project between the two countries' sovereign wealth funds and mediating a dispute between Libya and Saudi Arabia.[29])

Of Qatar's many efforts to expand its role on the world stage, Al Jazeera has remained the most visible actor, although the tone of its coverage remains reliably in sync with that of its royal Qatari sponsors. Shawn Powers and Eytan Gilboa observed: "First, Al Jazeera is not merely a transnational media organization, but also a network that acts and is treated as a powerful actor in international politics....Second, the network has adopted a political agenda relating both to the internal matters of the Arab world and to the external affairs of the rest of the world, primarily the West....Third, related to its status as an international political actor facing severe criticism from both inside and outside the Middle East, Al Jazeera has engaged in a widespread and thorough communications campaign to overcome the many controversies that it has been involved in."[30]

This is an instance of dual public diplomacies, with a government and a news organization reaching out to publics in distinct efforts but with shared purpose and linked agendas. Many nations use broadcasting as a public diplomacy tool, but the Qatar-Al Jazeera model stands out because the broadcaster maintains a separate public identity while it uses information as a tool in regional politics and carries out a de facto public diplomacy of its own.

China as Public Diplomacy Giant

China today conducts the world's most active and heavily funded public diplomacy. It has recently announced plans to invest the equivalent of US$6 billion in its international broadcasting programs. It sponsors more than 300 Confucius Institutes around the world (more than 70 in the United States) to offer training in Chinese language and culture. Politburo member Li Changchun stated that the Confucius Institutes are "an important channel to glorify Chinese culture, to help Chinese culture spread to the world," which is "part of China's foreign propaganda strategy."[31]

China hosted the 2008 Olympic Games and the Shanghai Expo of 2010. It has provided substantial financial aid to countries from which it purchases the natural resources it needs to sustain its growing economy. But does all this really benefit China? Jian Wang has written: "Many wonder just how effective China has been in capturing the 'hearts and minds' of the world. The story, so far, is mixed—with hits, duds, and many unknowns. For instance, the hosting of the Olympics has helped to broaden and reframe the international discourse about China, much to the benefit of the country's image. On the other hand, the vastly expanded Chinese state media has increased the production of news and information, but with little consumption by foreign publics. The influence of the Confucius Institutes seems subtle and will only be felt over time if the current operating model is to be sustained. However, the positive image China hopes to project is constantly overshadowed and undermined by negative headlines on the country's policies and governance. Just recently, the exposé of yet another spate of food safety scandals prompted Chinese Premier Wen Jiabao to lament in the Chinese media that, without strengthening culture and morality, 'China will never become a truly strong, respected nation.' "[32]

The results of a survey conducted in 2011 for the BBC World Service showed that negative opinions about China were substantial in wealthier nations, but China's popularity remained high in developing countries, especially in Africa.[33] This mix of opinions illustrates a difficulty that nations often face: success generates admiration, but also envy and fear. China is one of the major world powers of the twenty-first century and its embrace of public diplomacy indicates that it wants to capitalize on its emergence as an economic force, calm the uneasiness about its intentions, and be a leader of the global community. But, like the United States, China is learning that the more powerful a state becomes, the more skeptical global publics become about its motives. This makes crafting an effective public diplomacy strategy more challenging as well as more important.

Public Diplomacy in the Real-Time Era

In Benjamin Franklin's day, the public diplomat could do his job by talking to a few influential people and maintaining enough public visibility to be noticed by the decision-making elite. Given the slowness of communication between North America and Europe, Franklin was mostly on his own in terms of devising strategy for reaching his carefully selected but small audience and employing the tactics he needed to do so. He set his own pace, which was unhurried, but he was still able to serve American interests.

Today's public diplomat enjoys no such autonomy or leisure. Instructions arrive from many levels of bureaucracy, and every task is supposed to have been completed yesterday. With some in that bureaucracy still skeptical about public diplomacy's value (and/or not understanding what public diplomacy is), the public diplomat's work may not be accorded its rightful role as an integral part of larger diplomatic policy.

Public diplomacy strategies are increasingly driven by technology. Radio, long a mainstay of US outreach efforts, is being pushed aside in favor of Internet- and cell phone-based media. This might seem to make sense, but for such changeover to be effective, it cannot outpace the targeted public's own technological advances. If reliance on the Internet increases more quickly than the widespread usage of Internet, the tactic becomes self-defeating. Such moves may also stir up domestic political controversy. When the Voice of America decided in 2011 to shut down its shortwave radio service to China and shift the funding to digital technology, critics in congress and elsewhere claimed that this would deprive the Chinese of uncensored news.[34]

The emphasis on newer media is a function of the need for real-time public diplomacy. With so much of the world now receiving information from diverse sources at high speed, governments must be in this mix if they are to significantly affect the opinions of global publics.

Israel has been one of the pioneers in these matters, starting its official blog in 2006. This was a "lifestyle"-oriented product, and it was joined in 2007 by IsraelPolitik.org, which has addressed political issues. David Saranga, the Israeli foreign ministry official behind much of the early online effort, wrote that this blog "brings events in our area to worldwide attention, and adds Israel's viewpoint to political discussions from which it has often been missing." Saranga also initiated a "Citizens Press Conference" on Twitter because "we wanted to publicize Israel's official position, while allowing those who followed us to interact with the faces behind that information."[35]

The word often used by public diplomacy officialdom to describe this wielding of influence is "engagement," but that is a mushy term that lacks clear meaning. It can refer to something as ephemeral as the digital version of "pen pals"—useful, but in a minimal way—or to a broad-based online discussion forum that has a substantive effect on opinion formation. Engagement should not be seen as a strategy or a policy goal in itself; it is merely one tool among many. Public diplomacy requires multifaceted efforts designed to meet the particular political and cultural interests of the public for whom outreach is designed. This means, in part, that despite the infatuation with social media, public diplomacy should include direct personal contact whenever appropriate and feasible.

Considerable effort will be required to grapple with security and financial constraints, but projects based in tangible physical space, such as American libraries, remain valuable in ways that cyber connections cannot match. The audience reached individually by such ventures might not be as large as that which visits Facebook walls and reads Twitter feeds, but the qualitative value of the contacts might be more significant. The US embassy in Jakarta has received much attention for its digital campaigns, and its amassing of more than 300,000 Facebook followers is a tribute to the initiative of the embassy's staff. But what is the real nature of this connection? Are people really learning about the United States and its policies? Are their opinions being changed? As with any contact with the public, numbers in and of themselves mean little. This is particularly true given the casual ease with which "following" or "friending" or making other online connection can be done.

The US State Department is among the government organizations that have added "digital outreach" to their repertoires. By posting messages on Arabic, Urdu, Persian, and other Internet forums, the State Department project tries to connect directly to individuals who are part of target audiences, which is the essence of public diplomacy. The big question, to which there is not yet a definitive answer, is, does this technology-based approach work better, or at least as well, as more traditional contact techniques?

A report released in January 2011 by Stanford University found mixed results of the State Department's digital outreach venture. The report focused on the department's efforts related to President Obama's 2009 Cairo speech, and its principal findings included these:[36]

- The department states that the mission of the Digital Outreach Team (DOT) is "to explain U.S. foreign policy and to counter misinformation."

- The team members always identify themselves as working for the US State Department.
- Because members of the team must share their items with colleagues before posting them, the average response time was 2.77 days, which "makes it hard for readers to keep up with the points that they are specifically responding to."
- The DOT "does present an image of a government that is trying to engage with and listen to people directly (although this has been met with skepticism by some users who accuse them of being spies)."
- "When the DOT starts a thread about Obama's Cairo speech, it aims at making people think about the speech, putting it on the thought map."
- "If U.S. foreign policy toward the Middle East does not produce more than rhetorical change, public diplomacy 2.0 will not be able to alter perception of the USA in the region."

This final point sometimes is overlooked when the mechanics of message delivery receive inordinate attention and the substance of issues positions is treated only cursorily. Public diplomacy is a process, but it cannot be separated from policy. As Obama's short-lived surge in popularity in many Muslim countries indicated, deep-rooted skepticism about US intentions in the Arab world will limit even the most cleverly designed public diplomacy tactics.

In these matters, another concern should center on the question of intellectual influence afforded by use of new media, particularly social media as public diplomacy tools. To what extent are publics' opinions actually changing as a result of what they pick up from these media? Is there an intrinsic strength in this kind of messaging that makes the State Department Twitterer the equivalent of the Peace Corps volunteer? Do Tweets have the same impact in communities as a hands-on project, such as a new sanitation system?

High and low tech need not be—and should not be—mutually exclusive. The challenge for diplomats—the expeditionary diplomat in the field or the policymaker in the foreign ministry—is to create a public diplomacy that incorporates the modern without wholly abandoning the traditional.

PART III

SOCIAL MEDIA AND POLITICAL CHANGE

CHAPTER 6

THE PROMISE OF NETWORKS

The success of the Arab uprisings in 2011 was due in part to the ability to connect. Those who participated in one way or another could keep abreast of what was happening not only from conventional information sources but also from people plugged into social networks of various kinds.

The events of the Arab Awakening involved much more than "organizing," which includes face-to-face recruiting, logistical planning, liaison with other opponents of the regime, and more. These tasks can be arduous, but accomplishing them is a relatively straightforward process. Networks, however, are more complex—often not as visible or tangible as a street-based political operation. Networks rely on virtual and offline interpersonal connections that are sometimes local, sometimes global, and that typically involve multidimensional linkages between people, institutions, and parallel networks. A diagram of a network is multidimensional and often very intricate in the representations of these linkages.

Miriam Cooke and Bruce Lawrence have defined "networks" as "phenomena that are similar to institutionalized social relations, such as tribal affiliations and political dynasties, but also distinct from them, because to be networked entails making a choice to be connected across recognized boundaries."[1] This is a choice that is now more attainable than at any time in the modern past because of the technologies, especially digitized communication, that allow such connectivity. The networks are not limited to technological phenomena; rather, technology propels broader social networks. Also, the "boundaries" Cooke and Lawrence cited are not merely physical limits—such as borders between states—but rather social and cultural limits that Internet-based and other new media can transcend.

Amelia Arsenault offered another definition: "Networks may also be understood as building blocks. Different nodes can belong to multiple networks. An individual may serve as a node in a corporate network as well as in an otherwise separate political network. A network may also function as a node in a larger network. For example, a multilateral institution such as the United Nations operates as an organizational network comprised of formal nodes (e.g. UNESCO, UNDP, UNHCR, and its 192 country representatives). The UN simultaneously functions as a node in a larger multinational political network comprised of many formal and informal organizations (e.g. the UN, the United States government, NATO, the World Bank). The internal functioning (or malfunctioning) of the UN's organizational network may influence the larger international political network within which it serves as a node, and vice versa. Because networks can be constructed out of many smaller networks, it is generally more instructive to think of networks as embedded within a network of networks rather than one or several separate networks."[2]

Networks as theory became (not for the first time) networks in practice during 2011. Within Arab states and within the region, networks were crucial, bringing coherence and endurance to the Arab Spring. Understanding networks is essential for policymakers in this era when state-to-state diplomacy is only part of a nation's foreign relations. This is reflected in Manuel Castells's observation that "What we observe in the early years of the twenty-first century is simultaneously the crisis of the nation-state of the modern age and the return of the state under new organizational forms, new procedures of power making, and new principles of legitimacy."[3]

Networks and the Arab Awakening

In the context of the events of 2011, the chief product of networks was information that fostered political participation. Writing shortly before the Arab Awakening began, Clay Shirky observed, "As the communications landscape gets denser, more complex, and more participatory, the networked population is gaining greater access to information, more opportunities to engage in public speech, and an enhanced ability to undertake collective action. In the political arena ... these increased freedoms can help loosely coordinated publics demand change."[4]

Another characteristic of networks is their resilience. Charlie Beckett, writing about events in Tunisia and Egypt, noted that the movement driving the uprisings "was connected around nodal figures who all tended to resist conventional leadership roles. ... The diffuse, horizontal nature of these movements made them very difficult to break. Their diversity and flexibility gave them an organic strength. They were networks, not organizations."[5]

Dispersed but still connected; that is the basic geography of networks. It was a perfect model for the agents of change during the Arab Spring. Movement celebrities will always emerge, but for the day-to-day work of bringing down the governments of Ben Ali or Mubarak, or trying to have similar effect in other countries, more important than any individual was the breadth of mobilization that was enabled by networks. A contacted B; B in turn contacted C, D, and E; C then contacted F, G, and H; and D contacted I, J, and K; E contacted L, M, and N; and so on. L may have also contacted F, providing reinforcement to the original message from C, and F may have then sent it off in another direction. The connections move outward and inward simultaneously, creating an elaborate web such as the most diligent spider would weave.

This process is intricate, but not particularly complicated, even though the real numbers involved during the Arab Spring were exponentially greater than those in this little alphabetical exercise. Among social media tools, Facebook offers a good example of this process. Consider Facebook vis-à-vis television news. The television broadcast, although it may be disseminated to an audience of millions, reaches viewers individually and there is no back-and-forth communication—no real "connection." A Facebook posting, however, might initially reach a number (perhaps just a handful) of immediate friends, but then can be carried forward through Facebook by this initial audience to a far larger number of people who will read the message. Information transfer through social media networks is intrinsically participatory, as information consumers are also the primary distribution mechanisms. They decide what information they will post and report.

In military terminology, Facebook is a force multiplier; it can enhance the influence of a relatively small number of people, enabling them to have the reach and organizational capability of a far greater number. On the occasions that a Facebook page becomes widely popular, such as the "We Are All Khaled Said" Arabic page with well over a million fans, the network reaches enormous proportions as information is passed along by other social media, word of mouth, e-mails, or other means.

There are reasons that old-line Arab governments were so inept in their efforts at self-preservation. First, not just the heads of state but also their coteries of equally out-of-touch advisors had no understanding of what social media were and what they could do. The old-line politicos were still trying to adjust to the presence of Al Jazeera and other regional news organizations. Second, even once they figured out what was going on in terms of communication among their citizens, they were too slow and maladroit to keep up. All they could do was resort to drastic measures such as pulling the plug on the Internet, which is self-destructive for any country that is part of the global economy.

Lessons can be found in this experience for governments:

- The capacity of networks to dramatically influence politics should not be underestimated. Networks in themselves are not new, but the enhancement of their effectiveness through social and other new media is recent and ongoing... and increasing.
- Policymakers must be alert to social network organizing in its early stages if they want to either join or counter the political momentum that can build so quickly.
- The mission of a network should be analyzed carefully. Is it advocating incremental reform or immediate regime change? What are its prospects? How is its target likely to respond? Is the target using its own networks to push back, and, if so, how do the two sides' networks compare in terms of likely effectiveness?

Without considering such matters, third-party governments will lag behind developments. Staying on top of social networks' content should be part of the job of intelligence analysts and other officials involved in foreign policy planning.

Theory and Practice

Like the use of networks, theorizing about them is not new. As an academic topic, this has attracted top scholars and growing interest.

Among those intellectual leaders are Manuel Castells, based at the University of Southern California, and Anne-Marie Slaughter, of Princeton University, both of whom have written extensively about networks. They approach the issue from somewhat different perspectives, but the observations of each merit careful attention from policymakers who need to understand how communication-driven networks affect global affairs.

In his book *Communication Power,* Castells observed that "in the age of the Internet, individuals do not withdraw into the isolation of virtual reality. On the contrary, they expand their sociability by using the wealth of communication networks at their disposal, but they do so selectively, constructing their cultural world in terms of their preferences and projects, and modifying it according to the evolution of their personal interests and values. At the intersection of communalism and globalization, we find the culture of cosmopolitanism, or the project of sharing collective values on a planetary scale and thereby building a human community that transcends boundaries and specificity on behalf of a superior principle."[6] He adds that the *ummah,* the global community of Islam, is an example of this.

The concept is also applicable on a smaller scale both geographically and politically. Networks are the new communities. Castells wrote, "Appropriating the new forms of communication, people have built their own system of mass communication..." This, he added, "is in fact the reflection of the rise of a new form of socialized communication: mass self-communication. It is mass communication because it reaches potentially a global audience through the p2p [peer-to-peer] networks and Internet connection. It is multimodal, as the digitization of content and advanced social software, often based on open source that can be downloaded free, allows the reformatting of almost any content in almost any form, increasingly distributed via wireless networks. And it is self-generated in content, self-directed in emission, and self-selected in reception by many that communicate with many. We are indeed in a new communication realm, and ultimately in a new medium, whose backbone is made of computer networks, whose language is digital, and whose senders are globally distributed and globally interactive." This, observed Castells, "makes possible the unlimited diversity and the largely autonomous origin of most of the communication flows that construct, and reconstruct every second the global and local production of meaning in the public mind."[7]

Castells's analysis underscores the important fact that networks are much more than tactical creations used in political uprisings. What is happening, rather, is a rewiring of the central nervous system of civil society, with unprecedented empowerment of individuals who take advantage of communication tools.

Slaughter has examined the concept of networks as functions of states in the context of multilateral capabilities and responsibilities. In her book *A New World Order,* she writes: "The mantra of this book is that the state is not disappearing; it is disaggregating. Its component institutions—regulators, judges, and even legislators—are all reaching out beyond national borders in various ways, finding that their once 'domestic' jobs have a growing international dimension."[8] She notes that particularly for states that are rebuilding themselves, such as Iraq, it is important to be able to call upon networks of governments that can address problems "multilaterally rather than unilaterally, for reasons of legitimacy, burden sharing, and effectiveness."[9]

Reliance on networks, Slaughter contends, can strengthen standards of acceptable international behavior: "To the extent that the bond between members of a network is that they face common challenges and responsibilities, they are likely to strengthen norms of professionalism. It is likely that evident violations of those norms would quickly be transmitted across the network, raising the cost of those violations."[10]

This is the "new world order" that Slaughter envisions as a product of network connectivity—a redefined concept of "sovereignty" that eschews insularity and fosters new kinds of multinational cooperation.

Castells's and Slaughter's approaches to networks differ substantially but also are complementary in the sense that while Castells looks at "mass self-communication" and Slaughter examines more institutional concepts, they both appreciate how significantly networks alter the roles of individuals and nations in today's world.

In the face of this tectonic shift in the way the world works, policymakers should be more proactive in addressing the opportunities and challenges of networks. But they must also understand the evolutionary nature of network development and the resistance that will undoubtedly be mounted by some important global players.

Kenneth Weisbrode observed that Secretary of State Clinton had found that in moving toward a more networked global society, she was encountering roadblocks, most notably China. Clinton was finding out, wrote Weisbrode, that "the old ways of doing business—treaties, ambassadors, demarches, alliances, and the rest—may be useful after all." Expanding on this, Weisbrode cautioned that "better and faster communication is not a valuable end in itself, at least for diplomats. We need only recall the chaotic atmosphere during the recent United Nations climate conference in Copenhagen to fear the kind of disordered and disappointing result that can arise from the desire of everyone to be in the room and to be applauded everywhere at once—and to have the means of doing so.... Fortunately, a counter-trend in Copenhagen is also worth noting. Like-minded states, often neighbors, grouped together to pool their leverage: this was notable among some of the smaller and poorer states with the most at stake in addressing climate change. With care, such groupings may become the building blocks, rather than the spoilers, of global consensus."[11]

As Weisbrode indicated, a connection exists between networks, with their reliance on communication technologies, and the speed of diplomatic activity that may or may not be grounded in those technologies. Although negotiators edged closer to formulating significant climate-related rules at Copenhagen, the final outcome of the conference fell far short of what was needed in terms of addressing crucial issues related to global warming. This was largely attributable to the scientific and economic complexities of the matters being negotiated, but the situation in Copenhagen, as described by Weisbrode, also reflected some of the realities of postmodern diplomacy: cacophony superseding orderly negotiation, which was in this case offset somewhat by states individually asserting themselves and finding partners with whom to advance common interests.

In a more general sense, network-building depends on having shared interests and being willing to set aside differences in order to reach a common goal. This applies whether the issue at hand is addressing climate change or bringing down the Mubarak government. As for the mechanics of building a network, the tools vary according to the participants; individuals and nations will go about this process differently. For individuals and citizen groups, "liberation technology" is important. It has been defined by Larry Diamond as "any form of information and communication technology (ICT) that can expand political, social, and economic freedom," particularly digital ICT, and can "empower individuals, facilitate independent communication and mobilization, and strengthen an emergent civil society." He added, "Liberation technology enables citizens to report news, expose wrongdoing, express opinions, mobilize protest, monitor elections, scrutinize government, deepen participation, and expand the horizons of freedom." Diamond notes, however, that "not just technology but political organization and strategy and deep rooted normative, social, and economic forces" will prove determinative in terms of whether the "liberation" actually occurs.[12]

If all this seems somewhat underdeveloped as theory, that's because it is. Castells, Slaughter, and Diamond have addressed important issues related to the purposes, structure, and tools of networks, but knowledge about this field will remain somewhat speculative until there is wider recognition of the increasing ubiquity and potency of networks. Some policymakers and their governments are involved in networks without understanding them, but that will presumably change.

Theorists and policymakers have plenty to work with because examples of networks are not hard to find. Some have accomplished considerable good, while others are manifestations of evil.

Networks in Action

Among the characteristics of networks is the ability to organize a short-term, large manifestation of political sentiment that can be pulled together with great speed. Such was the case in the Philippines in 2001 during popular mobilization against the regime of President Joseph Estrada. Another function of a network is to displace a conventional "organization" by creating a dispersed, less hierarchical structure. Al Qaeda is an example of this.

The two cases examined here are by no means unique, but they provide a sense of how a network can become a potent political force.

Manila 2001

According to Howard Rheingold, Philippine President Joseph Estrada was "the first head of state in history to lose power to a smart mob."[13] Within four days in January 2001, millions of Filipinos were mobilized through digital technology to protest corruption in Estrada's government and to demand his ouster. This event became known as the first occasion on which the mobile phone played a determinative role in removing a head of government, and it was the progenitor of numerous mass reformist movements during the early years of the twenty-first century.[14]

Estrada, a well-known actor and ostensibly a populist, was elected president of the Philippines in 1998. Soon after taking office, he was accused of accepting bribes, mishandling public funds, and using illegal income to buy houses for his mistresses. By early 2001, impeachment proceedings were underway, reflecting public anger that was fueled in part by anti-Estrada information found on more than 200 websites and about 100 e-mail discussion groups. When the country's Senate refused to examine certain evidence as part of the impeachment process, "People Power II" began. This was the successor to the 1986 People Power movement that led to the end of Ferdinand Marcos's regime, but this later mobilization was made more feasible by a network connected by mobile phones. During People Power II, one SMS operator reported handling 45 million messages each day, almost double its usual load, and another operator handled 70 million messages during the week.[15] (The population of the Philippines in 2001 was about 78 million.)

The messages that were so widely spread ranged from logistics ("Meet at four o'clock at the church") to jokes about Estrada's personal life. As with later uprisings, such as the one in Tunisia in 2011, the Filipino movement succeeded in part because of larger political decisions, such as the military's siding with the protestors. Estrada quickly became isolated, without adequate institutional or popular support. As Castells et al. have pointed out, "the existence of a relatively weak state was a condition for the key role of the mobile phone and the Internet in this case."[16] In fairly short order, Estrada was escorted from the presidential palace by the military and his administration came to an end.

The greatest asset of the network in the Philippines case was its breadth and the speed with which mobilization messages could be conveyed. On the flip side of that, the greatest problem that Estrada faced was responding quickly enough to stay ahead of (or even abreast of) the events on the streets. During the following years,

mobile phones were invaluable to antigovernment political networks in South Korea, Ukraine, Ecuador, and elsewhere. Electronic
tools helped highly motivated protestors outmaneuver government
officials. In each case, the tools did not give birth to the movement,
but rather sped up a preexisting process by providing a means to
galvanize discontent.

It should be noted that these "popular" movements were built,
at least at first, among those who had access to the enabling technology, which means middle class and upward. The information
carried originally by digital networks can expand downward, in
socioeconomic terms (often aided by news media coverage), but the
networks first seek firm footing among a more homogeneous base
of support. That will change as the technology becomes less expen-
sive and more pervasive. When that happens, the traditional mass
media will become less consequential and the networks will reach a
size and breadth that will enhance their effectiveness. But as with all
political action, leaders who know how to use the available tools and
possess organizing skills are essential if a large public is to become
involved. Networks in themselves cannot replace those fundamental
skills.

This is not to denigrate the significance of networks per se. Their
dispersed, though not amorphous, nature makes them flexible and
difficult to suppress. They can facilitate a mass, public movement or
add resilience to a smaller, surreptitious venture.

Al Qaeda—More Than a Network?[17]

The world's best-known terrorist group, Al Qaeda, owes its survival partly to its ability to resist relying on a formal, hierarchical
structure and instead to develop a much less vulnerable network
model. Because Al Qaeda's operational leadership and the ranks of
its adherents are well dispersed, a case can be made that the killing
of Osama bin Laden in 2011 was useful but was more a symbolic
accomplishment than a devastating blow to Al Qaeda's capabilities.

That is because Al Qaeda is a supranational network that relies
on a mix of connectivity and geographical autonomy to accomplish
its goals. Because of its relative permanence, Al Qaeda might be
considered a mutation of a network, a "virtual state." It is something
of a confederation, with affiliates around the world (Al Qaeda in the

Islamic Maghreb, Al Qaeda in the Arabian Peninsula, and others) that run their own operations while still considering themselves to be parts of the greater whole and sharing a common purpose.

Al Qaeda as enemy creates problems of definition and policy, partly because it remains elusive as a physical opponent. It is not an enemy such as Germany and Japan were when the United States fought them during World War II. They were conventional nations with conventional military organizations, and they physically existed as territory that could be attacked and eventually occupied.

When the United States invaded Afghanistan in late 2001, US forces were attacking the Taliban that ruled the country, their guest Osama bin Laden, and fighters loyal to Al Qaeda. But Afghanistan was not the Al Qaeda homeland; there is no such thing, at least not in the traditional, physical sense. Even if Afghanistan were, over the long term, to become relatively peaceful, Al Qaeda would not necessarily be conquered. The real Al Qaeda homeland is vast and virtual, given cohesion by using cyber tools and new media rather than by having territory defined by borders.

Al Qaeda has troops; they exist in cells rather than divisions. It has a command structure, which—like much of the Internet-centric world—is decidedly nonlinear. For those who fight it, Al Qaeda may seem to be a scattered array of psychopaths operating under a common brand name. If that were true, they could be picked off one at a time and eventually the threat would be erased. But as a virtual state that has evolved from a more basic network, Al Qaeda possesses greater substance and resilience than might at first be seen, and it continues to evolve. Abdel Bari Atwan wrote that future organizational changes will "further take al Qaeda outside the scope and experience of international security forces. By converting al Qaeda into a set of guiding principles, an ideology, it transcends all national boundaries and makes affiliation or enfranchisement exceptionally easy."[18]

The US 9/11 Commission grappled with such matters, stating in its report: "National security used to be considered by studying foreign frontiers, weighing opposing groups of states, and measuring industrial might. To be dangerous, an enemy had to muster large armies. Threats emerged slowly, often visibly, as weapons were forged, armies conscripted, and units trained and moved into place. Because large states were so powerful, they also had more to lose.

They could be deterred. Now threats can emerge quickly. An organization like al Qaeda, headquartered in a country on the other side of the earth, in a region so poor that electricity or telephones were scarce, could nonetheless scheme to wield weapons of unprecedented destructive power in the largest cities of the United States.... Our enemy is twofold: al Qaeda, a stateless network of terrorists that struck us on 9/11; and a radical ideological movement in the Islamic world, inspired in part by al Qaeda, which has spawned terrorist groups and violence across the globe."[19]

A "stateless network" or a networked state? Faisal Devji observed that Al Qaeda is "non-geographical in nature, using the most disparate territories as temporary bases for its action. This makes it into an impossible enemy for the United States, because it exists beyond America's war-making potential." It is a new global category, wrote Devji, "with the geographical, financial, and technological mobility that defines globalization itself."[20]

As a matter of policy, Al Qaeda cannot be regarded as an "impossible enemy," but it is a difficult one. If Al Qaeda launches another major attack against the United States, Great Britain, or any other nation, how would the victim strike back? The supply of vulnerable "enemy" states is limited; Afghanistan and Iraq have already been checked off the list. And suppose it turned out that the attack was planned and directed by Al Qaeda operatives living in Paris or Rio de Janeiro or Montreal. Would a military response be feasible, or would the reaction be ratcheted down to the level of a police matter? That might be sensible, but would it be macho enough to be politically acceptable within the victim nation, assuming that the attack had caused large numbers of casualties? This hypothetical case illustrates how problematic dealing with networks, rather than conventional states, can be.

Part of addressing such matters involves understanding what Al Qaeda is and is not. It is often referred to as an "organization," which can be misleading because it conjures up images of conventional structure: a company such as General Motors or a fraternal group such as Rotary International. These organizations rely on clearly defined lines of authority and responsibility, with those at the bottom of the organizational structure—such as salespeople in the field or members of local clubs—linked and ultimately responsible to those at the top. Instructions and other information flow neatly, top to bottom. Such groups generally can be depicted by precise blueprints showing how they are organized.

But as Jason Burke observed, to view Al Qaeda "as a coherent and tight-knit organization, with 'tentacles everywhere' and with a defined ideology and personnel that had emerged as early as the late 1980s, is to misunderstand not only its true nature but also the nature of Islamic radicalism then and now."[21] Al Qaeda is not a corporation or a club. It is a political entity with a population—dispersed as it may be—that engages in financial transactions, communications activity, and paramilitary operations. With these characteristics and its global reach, Al Qaeda should be analyzed as a virtual state.

In terms of organizational design, the 9/11 Commission noted that as Al Qaeda evolved during the late 1990s it "relied heavily on the ideas and work of enterprising and strong-willed field commanders who enjoyed considerable autonomy."[22] A RAND study reported that before the US invasion of Afghanistan, Al Qaeda featured a combination of a hub-and-spoke structure, in which cells of operatives communicated with Osama bin Laden and his lieutenants in Afghanistan, and a wheel structure, where operatives communicated with each other without necessarily going through the leadership.[23]

After the fall of the Taliban and with bin Laden and others in the top echelon on the run, the structure became even more flexible. As Gabriel Weimann noted, "In the loose network structure, group members are organized into cells that have little or no contact with other cells or with a central control or headquarters. Leaders do not issue orders to the cells but rather distribute information via the media, websites, and e-mails that can be distributed and accessed anonymously. The advantage of this operational structure is that surveillance, penetration, or capture of operatives does not lead the intelligence agency to other cells or to the central control structure." Al Qaeda and other terrorist groups, added Weimann, "are loosely organized networks that rely less on hierarchical structure and more on horizontal networking. To varying degrees, many modern terrorist groups share the pattern of the loosely knit network: decentralization, segmentation, and delegation of authority."[24]

This reliance on networking gives Al Qaeda increased resilience. As a matter of counterterrorism strategy, the death of Osama bin Laden in 2011 was useful as a symbolic event and, in more practical terms, as removal of a principal strategist of global terrorism. But it did not damage Al Qaeda as severely as it would have if Al Qaeda had been organized as a conventional, hierarchical organization in which the CEO's removal would have a far more significant effect from top to bottom.

Virtual states possess considerable survivability, largely because of their incorporated multidimensional networks. Spanish politician and terrorism expert Gustavo de Aristegui identified four kinds of Al Qaeda networks. He reported that "first, there is the original network, the one that committed 9/11, which uses its own resources and people it has recruited and trained." Second is the "ad-hoc terrorist network, consisting of franchise organizations that al Qaeda created—often to replace ones that weren't bloody enough—in countries such as the Philippines, Jordan, and Algeria." Third, said Aristegui, is an umbrella network, "a strategic union of like-minded companies" tied to Al Qaeda by common purpose and funds provided by bin Laden. In the fourth network are the "imitators, emulators" who agree with Al Qaeda's program but have fewer financial connections to bin Laden. Members at this level, said Aristegui, carried out the 2004 Madrid bombings.[25]

Al Qaeda ventures range from the carefully planned, such as the 2001 attacks on the United States, to the opportunistic incidents such as the attempted firebombing of an American airliner in 2009. Al Qaeda has used its websites to urge its followers to make full use of the Internet. This message was on one of the sites: "We strongly urge Muslim Internet professionals to spread and disseminate news and information about the Jihad through e-mail lists, discussion groups, and their own Web sites. If you fail to do this, and our site closes down before you have done this, we may hold you to account before Allah on the Day of Judgment."[26]

In an evaluation of Al Qaeda's status in mid-2008, the *Economist* noted that "Al Qaeda is a terrorist organization, a militant network, and a subculture of rebellion all at the same time." Although Al Qaeda does have a physical presence in Pakistan, Somalia, and other places, the article posits that it is also a "'virtual caliphate' of cyberspace. The Internet binds together the amorphous cloud of jihadist groups, spreads the ideology, weaves together the 'single narrative' that Islam is under attack, popularizes militant acts, and distributes terrorist know-how. Because Al Qaeda is so dispersed, the fight against it has strained an international order still based on sovereign states."[27] Along similar lines, terrorism expert Daniel Benjamin warned against being "overly schematic" about Al Qaeda. He noted, "We like to draw organizational charts; they like to bomb things."[28]

Benjamin's observation underscores the need for policymakers to adapt to the cyber realities of dealing with terrorists who bring cold-blooded sophistication to their use of communication technologies. This is a savage aspect of globalization—terrorist groups' ability to take advantage of digital media's speed and connectivity to make the traditional protection of borders inconsequential and to menace the international community.

One approach to combating terrorists is to better understand the networks that terrorists use so adroitly. The US government has tried to identify linkages in large amounts of data, finding a suspected individual—such as one of the 9/11 terrorists—and examining the spider web of this person's contacts to see if patterns emerge. Perhaps other known terrorists will turn up on the grid and there will be common connections among them. Computer programs can perform such scans, but plenty of challenges remain in determining what the resulting information means.[29]

Might networks more indirectly bring an end to terrorism? Some theorists argue that when the Arab Awakening and similar movements open avenues to democracy, many people will be inclined to follow them rather than resort to terrorism.[30] That may be true, but suppose democracy falters, or even collapses, in some of the states such as those in the Arab world where expectations have risen so high. The networks on which hope was built could then become tools of bitter despair, and if new governments do not meet the needs and aspirations of the governed, networked anarchy could be a result.

Policymaking in the World of Networks

For individuals who want to participate in protest demonstrations, the mobile phone is probably the most valuable and commonly used tool. Online guides are available to help these participants use their phones wisely, offering suggestions such as these:

- understand the value of information that can be gathered, such as video of police activity;
- assess the risks involved if the data on your phone falls into the wrong hands;
- prepare for using your phone by backing up content, carrying a spare battery, paying ahead on a prepaid service plan, determining the extent of network coverage and such;
- evaluate potential physical dangers.[31]

A new wave of activists has been learning these skills during the past decade, with a huge surge in their numbers during 2011. Policymakers must take note of the entry into political life of these people, many of whom are young and whose presence will be felt for years to come. Just as they use new media devices to advance their own agendas, so too will new technologies spread their techniques—and perhaps their motivation—around the world.

This is the globalization of activism. What is new in this is not activism itself, but rather the speed at which it may spread. Much of this is benign, coming from people who sincerely want better lives for themselves and others, but there are also Al Qaeda and its derivatives, which have amassed an online library of terror techniques that is menacing in its scope and accessibility. There is a large supply of Internet-based "how to do it" material that covers bomb-making, assassination methods, and other topics that are designed for those who embrace a vicious kind of political action.

With all this material available, policymakers must recognize the capacity for both good and evil that is enhanced by digital technologies. The ability of the individual citizen to independently acquire information has transformed the world, drastically altering the relevance of fields such as journalism and diplomacy.

"News," in a broad sense, can be gathered by just about anyone without relying on the traditional institutions and practices of journalism. That may be a good thing in terms of democratizing this process, rendering the Rupert Murdochs of the world less influential. But it also means that a lot of garbage that would be filtered out by mainstream news organizations now enters and contaminates the public's information flow. It then may infect perceptions of public life. Still to be figured out is how to increase transparency and give people what they need as well as want to know in this new information environment, while avoiding the contamination of untruth. At the heart of this are issues related to networks—not the ABC, CBS, NBC kind, but those that are constructed by individuals. Twitter is a good example of networked information/news dissemination. It is no surprise that every major news organization is, in one way or another, seeking to capitalize on social media tools.

In many ways, developments in diplomacy parallel those in journalism. The insular world that diplomats for so long inhabited and controlled cannot survive amidst thriving popular networks. The WikiLeaks case typifies this change and should be considered on several levels. First was the matter of internal information security, which probably can be tightened considerably. But more significant was the broad dissemination of the leaked information. Networks such as those through which the WikiLeaks material passed will be increasingly common and governments' ability to stop the information flow will be increasingly unlikely. Once again, networks are overriding traditional mechanisms.

Successful networks are not limited to those who take to the streets and participate in movements that rely on nodal leadership. Diplomats are still grappling with ways to use networks without being overwhelmed by the participatory intensity they can engender. Foreign policy does not lend itself to crowdsourcing.

Although many networks operate outside the traditional center of politics and policy, their usefulness is bringing them into the mainstream where they continue to shape political action, journalism, and other fundamental aspects of society, almost always with real-time consequences.

CHAPTER 7

RIPPLE EFFECTS

In the continuum of politics, nothing is new; every act has its antecedents as well as successors. Further, nothing happens in a vacuum; others are always touched by even the most distant events.

The Arab Awakening of 2011 was much more than an event limited to the Arab world. It was a descendant of earlier political movements that utilized new technologies, and it has already proved to be a precursor of political disruption elsewhere.

Another constant: euphoria about democratization tends to be premature. Many tests await the Arab reformers, and inevitably some dreams will die. Furthermore, the offspring of positive events are not always positive themselves. In the United Kingdom during summer 2011, new communication technologies—and how government might restrict their use—were at the center of debate about widespread urban rioting and how to control it. The mini-uprisings in some British cities may have reflected years of social neglect, but as events played out on the streets they were nothing more than thuggery that happened to be aided by social media.

The following sections look backward and forward from the events in the Arab world in 2011. This is by no means a comprehensive survey of related occurrences, but these cases provide a look at the breadth of the political change taking place around the world.

Ukraine 2004

In the aftermath of the collapse of the Soviet Union and Communist hegemony in Eastern Europe, Ukraine was one of the former Soviet republics that moved uncertainly toward defining an independent identity. In 2004, after a virtual tie in a presidential election between the heavy-handed descendents of Soviet rule led by Prime Minister Viktor Yanukovych and a reform coalition led by Viktor Yushchenko, a run-off vote took place. Although exit polls showed the reformer Yushschenko winning handily, the official results gave the victory to Yanukovych.

The public was able to keep abreast of this discrepancy through the Internet and text messages, even though the state-controlled conventional media reported the apparently rigged outcome as fact. One report about these events stated that the new media serving as news deliverers "proved to be decisive. When the authorities announced Yanukovych's victory despite the fact that all independent exit poll results, as posted on opposition websites, indicated a decisive victory for Yushchenko, the Ukrainian people felt indignation and immediately started mass protests."[1]

People began to pour into the streets in peaceful demonstrations. One writer who was there observed that "throngs of protestors were out in the bitter cold, making their voices heard. In offices, everybody took shifts. Some would stay behind and work while the others went out to the protests, then return and allow their coworkers to join in. Outside the election commission, every car passing by would honk its horn, creating a 24-hour cacophony to disturb those complicit in the fraud. At the Rada, Ukraine's Parliament, as at all government buildings, protestors maintained a 24-hour vigil."[2] Many of those who were protesting wore orange clothing, and this became dubbed "the Orange Revolution."

The protestors relied heavily on the Internet and mobile phones. One report stated: "First, the Internet allowed for the creation of a space for dissenting opinions of 'citizen journalists' in an otherwise self-censored media environment. Second, pro-democracy activists used the convergence of mobile phones and the Internet to coordinate a wide range of activities including election monitoring and large-scale protests."[3]

In addition to aiding organization of the protests and keeping people in Ukraine informed about what was going on, the Internet proved to be an effective way of reaching the outside world. Volodymyr Lysenko and Kevin Desouza wrote that "the Internet was used to overcome government-imposed limitations on [the opposition's] broadcasts' geographical reach, and thus provide important alternative information to a wider range of people. This was especially effective in reaching a foreign audience in developed countries, which already had widespread and affordable broadband Internet access and was able to watch the Orange Revolution live 24/7" on the Web.[4]

In retrospect, the Orange Revolution may have been the first such event to have been organized primarily through the Internet. Joshua Goldstein wrote that "these events marked an important crossroads where the emergence of open networks and rapid political change converge. Ukraine's digital revolutionary stage drew on several emerging tools. These tools had a broad range of uses, from coordination of activists via SMS to the development of an independent online media, to website discussion boards for activists to share best practices and make detailed reports of election fraud."[5]

Although the Orange Revolution occurred early in the history of new media-assisted uprisings, its organizers possessed a sophisticated understanding of how to build effective networks. One of these organizers, Andriy Ignatov, later noted: "In order to cover a larger audience, we had to attract our target audience from people who are usually better networked than the rest. We strived to reach investigative journalists, human rights lawyers, entrepreneurs, and students. In short, we wanted to reach the most networked people in Ukraine."[6]

The protests achieved their goal. The run-off results were declared invalid by Ukraine's Supreme Court, which ordered a new vote. This time, Yushchenko won by an 8 percentage point margin.

Since then, Ukraine's politics have remained tumultuous, but the Orange Revolution showed that at least for this one country at this particular time, the democratic promise of the post-Soviet era could be fulfilled.

Obamamania 2008

"Yes we can!" As a political slogan chanted at rallies, it was compelling, and when typed on the keyboard of a smartphone, a laptop, or even a stodgy old desktop computer, the words transformed the new frontier of American politics—cyberspace.

In 2008, Barack Obama rode a glorious wave while his opponents debated whether they should even get into the water. In findings released in June 2008, just midway through the campaign year, the

Pew Internet & American Life Project reported that 46 percent of all American adults were using the Internet, e-mail, or phone text messaging for political purposes. More specifically,

- 40 percent of all Americans (Internet users and nonusers alike) got news and information about the campaign via the Internet;
- 19 percent were going online once a week or more to engage politically, and 6 percent did so daily;
- 23 percent said they were receiving e-mails urging them to support a particular candidate or discuss the campaign at least once a week;
- 10 percent said they were using e-mail to participate in the political debate at least once weekly;
- 10 percent used social networking sites for political activity;
- 35 percent had watched online campaign videos (more than triple the number during the 2004 presidential race);
- 8 percent of Internet users (representing 6 percent of all adults) made a financial contribution to a candidate online.[7]

During the fall general election campaign, Obama far outdistanced his Republican opponent, John McCain:

- Obama had more than 2 million American supporters on Facebook, while McCain had just over 600,000. (This continued Obama's strength during his primary run against Hillary Clinton, during which his Facebook page had attracted more than 250,000 fans, while Clinton's had only 3,200.)
- On Twitter, Obama had 112,000 Tweeting supporters, while McCain had 4,600.
- On YouTube, Obama's supporters uploaded more than 1,800 videos onto the BarackObama.com channel, which attracted 97 million video views, while McCain's channel had 330 videos and 25 million video views.[8]

These statistics reflecting the rise of new media signaled a change in American politics as profound as that which occurred in 1960, when John F. Kennedy showed the effectiveness of television as a campaign tool. Campaigning is about reaching people—on their doorsteps, on their television screens, and now on their computer monitors and mobile phones. Some of the most effective voter contact has always come from family members or friends. Talk around the dinner table, at the water cooler, or at a social event can reinforce, and sometimes change, opinion and voting behavior. Now the person who cares about an election can sit at home and contact dozens, or maybe hundreds, of friends in a few moments while using an e-mail list.

Sometimes we don't realize how connected we are. We have all those names on our phone or our computer, and we can easily send an "I hope you'll watch this" note with a link to a YouTube video. In doing so, we would have accomplished a feat of campaigning that would have earned the respect of a political boss of several generations ago.

Although Barack Obama availed himself of the newest ways to reach voters, he did not divorce himself entirely from old-style politics. He used much of the money he raised online to buy television advertising time, and many of the volunteers recruited online were dispatched to campaign door-to-door—basic retail electioneering.

The transitional nature of the 2008 US campaign was evident in several ways. Candidates found that their speeches or even off-hand comments were rocketing around the online world before they had even finished talking. Almost every gaffe was picked up by someone with a mobile phone microphone or camera and quickly made available for the public to see. The gatekeeping function of the mainstream press mattered far less than it had in the past. There were too many gates through which information could pass, and many of them were wedged open. Almost every bit of political information—including the trivial, unfair, and untrue—showed up in some form on new media venues. This topic will be explored further later in this chapter in the context of what journalists' responsibilities should be. Should they deliver as "news" whatever information is dropped onto the information conveyor belt, or should they discriminate based on a carefully designed process of evaluation?

As both major parties prepared for the 2012 presidential race, Republicans vowed to catch up to the Democrats in social media use, particularly in the sense of fully integrating digital strategy into the central campaign effort. Meanwhile, the Obama reelection campaign was determined to keep its high-tech advantage, and so was in high gear by spring 2011. In April, Obama announced his bid for reelection with e-mail and text message blasts, posts on Twitter, a YouTube video, and an app to connect his supporters and his Facebook friends to his campaign website. In announcing, Obama asked simply, "Are you in?" Later that month, Obama's Facebook page featured this 30-second YouTube video: "Hi everybody. I just want to take a minute to invite you to a town hall meeting on the economy that I'm holding at Facebook's headquarters this Wednesday, April 20. It is going to be live-streamed, and I will answer questions from folks across the country." By the next day, more than 22,000 people had signed up.[9]

The Obama campaign was unlike the Arab uprisings of 2011 in that it operated within the rubric of conventional American electoral politics. But the lessons of localizing and even personalizing the quest for votes on such a large scale demonstrated that campaigning could be restructured by innovatively using communication technologies. By proving that change was possible—in this instance the election of the first person of color to be president of the United States—Obama's 2008 campaign stirred the embers of hope elsewhere, and they helped ignite the Arab Awakening three years later.

United Kingdom 2011

Following a peaceful march on August 6, 2011, in London to protest the fatal police shooting of a 29-year-old black man, rioting broke out in the Tottenham area of London. During the next few days, riots erupted in other parts of London as well as in Manchester, Birmingham, and elsewhere. At least 5 people died and more than 3,000 were arrested.

At first glance, the British riots had little in common with the Arab uprisings other than their timing. The protest against alleged police misconduct was a significant political matter, as was the frustration of minorities who saw themselves as an increasingly marginalized underclass. But beyond such underlying causes, any political comparison with the Arab Spring breaks down. The wanton looting and arson that occurred bore no resemblance to events in the Arab states. The British rioters did, however, make use of mobile technologies, notably Blackberry Messenger, in ways that helped the disorder spread. In the United Kingdom, Blackberry has 37 percent of the teenage mobile phone market, and Blackberry Messenger is popular because it allows free messaging to individuals or to all of someone's Blackberry-toting contacts at once.[10]

Some British officials called on Research in Motion (RIM), the Canadian firm that makes Blackberry, to suspend its messaging service to keep the rioters from communicating with one another. Prime Minister David Cameron said the government itself should consider blocking social media use by those who were engaged in violence or disorder.[11] In a speech to Parliament, Cameron said: "Everyone watching these horrific actions will be struck by how they were organized via social media. Free flow of information can be used for good, but it can also be used for ill. And when people are using social media for violence, we need to stop them. So we are working with the police, the intelligence services, and industry to look at whether it would be right to stop people communicating via these websites and services when we know they are plotting violence, disorder, and criminality. I have also asked the police if they need any other new powers."[12]

Cameron seemed to have adopted the notion that social media *cause* disorder. That is as much in error as labeling the Arab Awakening "the Twitter revolution" and attributing power to the tools, rather than to the people who wielded them. Without in any way justifying the violence that flared in the United Kingdom, one can still identify real socioeconomic causes for the disorder. Although social media can serve as multipliers, merely having Blackberry phones did not cause the riots.

Just six months earlier, in a speech in Kuwait, Cameron had offered a very different view of new media such as those phones: "It belongs to a new generation for whom technology—the Internet and social media—is a powerful tool in the hands of citizens, not a means of repression. It belongs to people who've had enough of corruption, of having to make do with what they're given, of having to settle for second best."[13]

In the Arab world, people who had just come through their own uprisings intently watched events in Britain and appeared to feel little kinship with the rioters. One Egyptian blogger wrote, "Egyptians and Tunisians took revenge for Khaled Said and Bouazizi by peacefully toppling their murdering regimes, not stealing DVD players."[14]

As for giving police "new powers," as Cameron offered, that is a door that once opened might be difficult to close. When law enforcement agencies begin using data from communication companies, a chilling effect on all users becomes inevitable. Among possible police uses of information from RIM or service providers would be traffic information: who messaged whom and from where. This might be matched up with closed-circuit (CCTV) video and help police give names to the faces of rioters.[15] Besides police use of communication data, wrote Evgeny Morozov, "cyber vigilantes" were studying Facebook, Flickr, and other social networks to see if they could recognize people in the online images from the riots.[16]

While some politicians and journalists were quick to blame social media for the intensity and breadth of the rioting, Ramesh Srinivasan noted that to blame the British disorder on Blackberry or Facebook or any other media tool would be counterproductive. "Over-generalizing social media's role," he wrote, "could do more to harm our understanding of an uprising than help it." He added that when a government targets Blackberry, for instance, "we ignore the powerful economic and political grievances that drive discontent. With or without these technologies, people will ultimately stand up and speak their minds. If we continue to focus on technologies rather than people, we risk ignoring the source of their grievances and the more complex, organic networks by which they choose to communicate."[17]

Morozov also warned that democratic governments should be careful about providing apparent validation to China and other authoritarian states that have imposed tough controls on social media. He wrote that Western politicians who propose controls fail to see that "such measures can also affect the fate of dissidents in places like China and Iran. Likewise, how European politicians handle online anonymity will influence the policies of sites like Facebook, which, in turn, will affect the political behavior of those who use social media in the Middle East."[18]

As if to reinforce Morozov's point, as the London riots were winding down San Francisco's Bay Area Rapid Transit (BART) authority disabled mobile phone service in four underground stations to hinder demonstrations that had been planned to protest the fatal shooting of a man by BART transit police officers. BART alleged that the demonstrations "could lead to platform overcrowding and unsafe conditions," and noted that "organizers planning to disrupt BART service stated they would use mobile devices to coordinate their disruptive activities and communicate about the location and number of BART police." A BART spokesperson said, "It really is just a cost-benefit analysis of where your freedom of speech begins to threaten public safety."[19]

The legal issues arising from this incident are numerous and complex, but it is safe to say that the notion of applying a "cost-benefit analysis" as a means of regulating speech will provoke much debate. Governments of all political persuasions tend to prefer to follow the path of least resistance in doing their work, and that path may veer toward controlling media that enhance citizens' power vis-à-vis that of government. This is a trend that could pick up momentum and lead to serious consequences for those in both free and not-so-free countries who see communication as a way to redress wrongs and stimulate reform.

A final note about the British riots: after the violence subsided, volunteers used Facebook and Twitter to mobilize people to help clean up the mess that the disorder had left behind. A newly created Twitter account, @riotcleanup, attracted more than 70,000 followers in two days, and people with brooms and shovels poured into riot-stricken neighborhoods to help however they could. This was social media at its constructive, community-building best.[20]

Journalism

In both symbolic and practical ways, the global public's vastly expanded access to foreign policy information took shape in late 2010 with the release of the WikiLeaks documents—250,000 cables transmitted between the US State Department and 270 US diplomatic stations around the world. The *New York Times* and several news organizations outside the United States were presented with these documents and given the opportunity to publish them. They had been obtained by WikiLeaks, which describes itself as "a non-profit media organization dedicated to bringing important news and information to the public. We provide an innovative, secure and anonymous way for independent sources around the world to leak information to our journalists. We publish material of ethical, political and historical significance while keeping the identity of our sources anonymous, thus providing a universal way for the revealing of suppressed and censored injustices."[21]

Possibilities for disseminating information had expanded immeasurably since the leak of the Pentagon Papers in 1971. Those documents, which were part of a US government study of the relationship between the United States and Vietnam between 1945 and 1967, could only have reached a large public through mainstream news outlets. The *New York Times,* the *Washington Post,* and 15 other US newspapers published parts of the documents, and other news organizations then picked up the story, to the great irritation of many US government officials.

In 2010, the Internet was at hand to provide a comfortable home for WikiLeaks, although the impact of the material was amplified when traditional news providers carried it. On the first day on which it published WikiLeaks material, the *New York Times* also published a "Note to Readers" explaining its decision to reveal the material. It said: "The *Times* believes that the documents serve an important public interest, illuminating the goals, successes, compromises and frustrations of American diplomacy in a way that other accounts cannot match." Noting that about 24,000 of the documents were marked "secret" and/or "noforn," meaning not to be shared with other countries, the *Times* said it had excised material "that would endanger confidential informants or compromise national security." In addition, the newspaper said it had allowed US officials to review the material before publication and had acceded to some of the government's requests to cut out particular items.

The *Times* said that an important reason to publish the material was that "the cables tell the unvarnished story of how the government makes its biggest decisions, the decisions that cost the country most heavily in lives and money. They shed light on the motivations—and, in some cases, duplicity—of allies on the receiving end of American courtship and foreign aid.... As daunting as it is to publish such material over official objections, it would be presumptuous to conclude that Americans have no right to know what is being done in their name."[22]

This case illustrates one of those intersections of journalism and diplomacy where the parties recognize they have both shared and divergent interests. In this instance, the government wanted to preserve secrecy and the news media wanted to reveal information; this reflects the healthy adversarial tension that is the norm for news media–government relations. But, as the *Times* statement indicated, the newspaper's editors also recognized their quasi-political role in giving the Obama administration advance warning about the forthcoming publication and also offering to consider requests for redactions from the material. The journalists understood, however, that their decision making about what the public would and would not see was limited, because they knew that WikiLeaks intended to publish the entire archive on its own website, where it would be available to everyone who had Internet access.

The *Times's* engaging in back and forth with US government officials slowed down the process a bit; the Obama administration had time to alert its diplomats that the WikiLeaks documents would soon be available for public perusal. Given that some of the cables included derogatory comments about foreign officials, allegations of corruption, and other controversial items, the US representatives in the field had time to do some anticipatory fence-mending. There is certainly no assurance, however, that such a grace period will always be available. The WikiLeaks organization or anyone else could deliver a huge document dump onto the Internet and all affected parties would need to scramble to try to assess and contain damage. In September 2011, the master file containing the entire collection of 251,000 American diplomatic cables became available online. It included everything from the private phone number of the Queen of the Netherlands to information about China's nuclear power plants.[23] Once again, US diplomats needed to repair damaged relationships.

This is an aspect of real-time diplomacy that foreign policy practitioners must learn to live with. Major news organizations such as the BBC, CNN, or the *New York Times* have close enough ties to governments that they may engage in conversation or at least provide a short-term alert before publishing material that might have significant diplomatic or security repercussions. But there are plenty of real or quasi-news organizations that would see no need to contact the government in advance and would probably enjoy the consternation produced by surprise.

In another case, in early 2011 Al Jazeera and the *Guardian* released "The Palestine Papers," which illustrated far greater flexibility on the part of Palestinian Authority (PA) negotiators in their dealings with Israel than the public had known about. This created an anti-PA backlash from Hamas and others who believed that the

PA was selling out its constituents. Al Jazeera had acquired, from a Palestinian Authority source, more than 1,600 documents, including e-mail messages and maps. PA reactions ranged from evasive political maneuvering to counterattacking in the classic spirit of "kill the messenger." At the heart of the PA's angry frustration was the fact that the accuracy of the leaked material could not be successfully challenged. The PA's situation was made worse by its being unprepared to respond with the speed that the real-time news cycle demands. PA spokespersons contradicted themselves and generally looked inept, and the only thing that worked in their favor was that the story was quickly overshadowed by events in Egypt.[24]

WikiLeaks and the Palestine Papers were examples of the kind of news dissemination that the public will increasingly demand. "Transparency" has moved from being a distant ideal to becoming an expectation, and its absence will increasingly trigger public protest. The desire for transparency can be fulfilled by a combination of the efforts of traditional journalists and independent diggers such as those who retrieved the WikiLeaks documents.

Part of this change reflects an evolution in the definition of "journalism," which those who appreciate the profession's ideals of fairness and accuracy cannot afford to ignore. People who were once dismissed as polemicists or propagandists now have more to work with; using digital media tools, they can find and distribute information that can reach large audiences. They do so without necessarily running it through the journalistic process of corroboration and context-building.

Policymakers who think they understand how journalists work will also need to adjust their views of what constitutes the news media. Information dissemination is not, in itself, journalism, but unless the public recognizes this distinction, those who make and implement policy will need to be more inclusive in how they approach "the media."

None of this is to say that traditional journalism is irrelevant. Along with the influx of satellite television channels and new venues powered by social media tools, a sizable, dedicated profession continues its efforts to serve the public (and turn a profit) by delivering news. Their role becomes more significant in this era of globalization, which can be characterized as a time when economic forces and new technologies are reordering connections among the world's citizens. Columbia University president Lee Bollinger wrote of this: "We need institutions designed to help us understand, tame, and channel these largely positive forces, and a free and independent global press is one such institution. More than anything, we need a change in consciousness—to envision the problem we must solve as not only a matter of securing human rights for peoples but also securing the information and ideas we need to govern effectively in an increasingly integrated world."[25]

A sometimes overlooked facet of the Arab Spring was the assertion of those in the rising generation that they have a *right* to receive honest and complete information. They will expect this right to be defended by journalists and upheld by governments. Particularly because of the growing public interest in this right, advancing it should become a central element of global diplomacy.

★   ★   ★

As the examples cited in this chapter illustrate, the Arab Awakening was not an isolated event, but rather was part of a continuum of change enhanced by information and communications technology. This change extends well beyond politics; journalism is just one of the fields that have been substantially altered by the mix of technological capabilities and societal expectations. Diplomats find themselves dealing with the full scope of this sociopolitical evolution that touches their work in so many ways.

Looking ahead, as the following chapter will do, reveals new tests that await: ensuring Internet freedom; addressing the future of the Arab world and the relationship between Muslim and non-Muslim societies; and further adapting diplomacy to the exigencies of this new era.

CHAPTER 8

LOOKING AHEAD

Like the erratic flight path of a moth, the course of international politics often seems to be an example of purposeful aimlessness. Wise diplomats try to anticipate trends and prospective events, but they recognize that any grand strategy can be undermined by the elusiveness of predictability. If anyone were to say, "I knew the Tunisian, Egyptian, and Libyan regimes would fall in 2011," that person's hubris would be scoffed at. But if someone said, "Given the economic and social conditions in Tunisia, Egypt, and Libya, and given the new communication tools that allow people better understanding of the world and better ability to connect with one another, I knew the regimes there were bound to fall at some point," that person's claim to prescience might be greeted with skepticism, but at least the prediction would be considered plausible.

Diplomacy is not a guessing game, but nor should it be so wrapped up in events of the moment that possible outcomes down the road are ignored. One lesson of 2011 is that the pace of events increases along with the rate of information flow. This means policymakers must fine-tune their operating procedures to improve their ability to move quickly but still wisely, and to anticipate the shifting degrees of importance of specific issues.

For proponents of democracy, the 2011 Arab Awakening provided reason to applaud the influential, if not determinative, role of social media in particular and Internet-based information flows more generally. Along with satellite television, these new media transformed the intellectual landscape in the Arab world and helped offset the brutish force on which governments there had so long relied. Plenty of political leaders, however, consider democracy to be anathema and see the events of early 2011 as a warning. To improve their regimes' chances of survival, they are certain to try to design ways to control these media. The resulting struggle will be one of the major global political battles of the coming years.

Internet Freedom

In a speech on February 15, 2011, just four days after Hosni Mubarak stepped down, US secretary of state Hillary Rodham Clinton addressed the significance of the Internet and the need to protect access to it: "The Internet has become the public space of the 21st century—the world's town square, classroom, marketplace, coffee-house, and nightclub. We all shape and are shaped by what happens there, all 2 billion of us and counting. And that presents a challenge. To maintain an Internet that delivers the greatest possible benefits to the world, we need to have a serious conversation about the princi-ples that will guide us, what rules exist and should not exist and why, what behaviors should be encouraged or discouraged and how. The goal is not to tell people how to use the Internet any more than we ought to tell people how to use any public square, whether it's Tahrir Square or Times Square. The value of these spaces derives from the variety of activities people can pursue in them, from holding a rally to selling their vegetables, to having a private conversation. These spaces provide an open platform, and so does the Internet. It does not serve any particular agenda, and it never should. But if people around the world are going to come together every day online and have a safe and productive experience, we need a shared vision to guide us."[1]

This was Clinton's second major speech about Internet freedom (she delivered the previous one in January 2010) and it underscored her commitment to the "freedom to connect," which she tied to other fundamental rights: "The rights of individuals to express their views freely, petition their leaders, worship according to their beliefs—these rights are universal, whether they are exercised in a public square or on an individual blog. The freedoms to assemble and associate also apply in cyberspace. In our time, people are as likely to come together to pursue common interests online as in a church or a labor hall."[2]

The State Department had also begun a series of Twenty-First-Century Statecraft initiatives that used Internet technologies to make statecraft more innovative and brought private sector technology resources into government programs. This policy stance is noteworthy in that it reflects the relatively high priority the US government has assigned to Internet freedom and related issues.

Given the strenuous efforts of some governments, such as those of Iran and China, to infringe on Internet freedom, the US commitment, if it is to mean anything, must be backed up by an assertive defense of Internet use that goes beyond statements of principles. This will not be easily done, because some countries have devoted considerable effort to imposing "soft" controls—those that do not rely solely on blockage or other direct interference with access. China has fostered the growth of local sites, such as Youku and QQ, which offer nonpolitical content and community-building tools popular with users. One 2011 study, conducted by Harvard University's Berkman Center for Internet & Society, found that "there are multiple reasons Chinese users choose Youku and QQ over YouTube and Facebook. China's aggressive blockage of these sites is one. The high quality of the Chinese sites and their linguistic accessibility to Chinese users is another. National pride and a desire to use local products may be a third. But the result of these intersecting factors has been the thorough segregation of the Chinese Internet from the rest of the world."[3]

In this same report, researchers concluded that the struggle against government control of the Internet had become more of an uphill battle. For years, circumvention tools, such as web proxies and Virtual Private Network (VPN) services, provided ways to detour around government-imposed cyber blockades, but governments have now found ways to offset those circumvention efforts. The report's authors wrote: "Four years ago, we were reasonably sure that the developers of circumvention tools were winning the match against government censors. Not only is victory in that match less assured now, the entire playing field has changed, and new technologies of control are far harder to defend against than national Internet filtering."[4]

In the face of government-imposed blocking, however, circumvention mechanisms remain an important remedy. Although these tools are used by only a small number of people, the Berkman researchers pointed out that "the impact of the tools can be greatly magnified if core populations of highly connected and influential people use the tools and distribute the information they gather or post through the tools to a much wider audience."[5]

Regimes wanting to control Internet use by their political opponents are still learning. Jim Cowie, chief technology officer of the Internet assessment company Renesys, wrote: "Using denial of Internet access as a political weapon during crisis events is all about timing and messaging. Mubarak waited too long to implement his blackout, and then let it run past the point where the damage to the Egyptian economy and the cost of international outrage exceeded the dwindling benefits to the regime. In the end, all the Egyptian government accomplished was to attract the sort of sympathetic attention and message support from the Internet community that is pure oxygen to a democratic opposition movement." Cowie also noted that in the future governments are likely to try "bandwidth throttling," which slows down page downloads and video streaming, keeping the Internet available, but making it less useful.[6]

More insidious than technical obstructions are political pressures. In the face of legal and physical risk, bloggers selectively self-censor themselves. According to the Berkman researchers, "Internet censorship may not be solely, or even primarily, about blocking access to international content," but rather may be based on simply "suggesting that Internet connections are subject to surveillance."[7] This threat can stifle freedom of expression just as effectively as actual blocking mechanisms do.

In some countries bloggers live with the daily possibility of a knock on the door and a quick trip to a jail cell. Even in postuprising Egypt, freedom to blog was constrained by the army. In April 2011, when blogger Maikel Nabil Sanad accused the military of remaining loyal to Hosni Mubarak, he was sentenced to three years in prison. An army spokesperson said that criticism "for the public good" would be allowed, but not "questioning the intentions" of the army.[8] During the tense days just two months before, Egyptians in Tahrir Square had chanted, "The military and the people go hand in hand." The trust and goodwill that existed then had offered hope, but this quickly dissipated.

★   ★   ★

Writing about the unending conflict in Somalia, Eliza Griswold reported about a radio station that had been crippled by attacks designed to knock it off the air. She wrote: "No one wanted a free press. Ignorance served all parties better."[9] There are those throughout the world who have no qualms about choking off the flow of information as a means of grasping and keeping power. Those who do not want a free press certainly do not want a free Internet.

Like any other kind of liberty, Internet freedom will not come easily. The battles about it will become more sophisticated as autocratic governments increasingly view the control of online information as essential to their self-preservation. Efforts to achieve and maintain this freedom will proceed on two levels: the technological competition between those who impose barriers and those who find ways around them; and the political contest between those who see control as a matter of state sovereignty and those who want to establish an international norm of openness.

The determinative factor may be the persistence of those who value the intellectual communities of interest that access to the Internet encourages. These are the people who took heart from what they read in Tweets from Tunis and saw on YouTube videos from Cairo, who found colleagues on Facebook and discovered new ideas in blogs. Knowing that their struggles are not over, they might embrace Internet freedom as their next cause.

Islam and the World

The title of the Pew Research Center's July 2011 report states the situation clearly: "Muslim-Western Tensions Persist."

The report summarizes its principal findings this way: "Muslim and Western publics continue to see relations between them as generally bad, with both sides holding negative stereotypes of the other. Many in the West see Muslims as fanatical and violent, while few say Muslims are tolerant or respectful of women. Meanwhile, Muslims in the Middle East and Asia generally see Westerners as selfish, immoral, and greedy—as well as violent and fanatical."[10]

One of the issues at the heart of Muslims' dissatisfaction with their own state of affairs is the persistent lack of prosperity in predominantly Muslim countries. Government corruption and US and Western policies receive a large part of the blame, but Muslims increasingly cite the absence of democracy as a major factor. Between

2006 and 2011, the percentage of respondents who said "lack of democracy" was responsible for Muslim states' lack of prosperity rose from 32 to 48 percent in Egypt, from 28 to 42 percent in Jordan, and from 35 to 49 percent in Indonesia (with smaller percentages in other Muslim nations).[11]

Another example of the divide can be seen in how people identify themselves. In Western, predominantly Christian, countries, when asked whether they identified themselves primarily by citizenship or by religion, respondents stated that nationality came first in every country except the United States: 70–23 nationality over religion in Germany; 53–22 in Spain; 63–21 in Britain; 68–19 in Russia; 90–8 in France; and 46–46 in the United States. (The respondents in these countries were Christians only.) In Muslim countries, however, religion was rated more significant everywhere except in the Palestinian Territories and Lebanon: in Pakistan, 3 percent cited nationality while 94 percent cited being a Muslim; in Jordan, 24 percent Jordanian, 65 percent Muslim; in Turkey, 21–49; in Egypt, 31–46; in Indonesia, 35–40; in the Palestinian Territories, 43–40; and in Lebanon, 36–28. (The respondents in these countries were Muslims only.)[12]

This polling was done in March and April 2011 (except in Pakistan, where the survey was conducted in May), in the aftermath of many of the most dramatic moments of the Arab Spring. Even with greater appreciation for democracy, Muslims retain a firm grasp on their Islamic identity, and Western policymakers who want to work with Muslim states had best recognize the pervasive power of Islam.

Among many in the West, there is condescension toward this relatively young religion. Some would make the case that if Islam, which is about 1,400 years old, is compared to Christianity in the fifteenth century—the aftermath of the Crusades and when the Inquisition continued—Islam might "mature" and evolve. But into what? Something non-Muslims are more comfortable with? A five-year study conducted by the Program on International Policy Attitudes (PIPA), which is based at the University of Maryland, found that many Muslims believe that "America is seeking to impose its Western secular model of governance and to eradicate the role of Islam in the public sphere. Since to Muslims Islam is, by definition, meant to be in the public sphere, American efforts are seen as seeking to undermine Islam itself."[13]

The Pew report states, "Muslims continue to believe there is widespread hostility toward them in the West." Americans are seen as being particularly hostile—more so than Europeans in most of the Muslim countries surveyed. In the Palestinian Territories, Turkey, and Pakistan, more than 70 percent of respondents said that they think most or many Americans are hostile toward Muslims.[14] Further, according to the PIPA research, "Western cultural products are seen as seductively undermining Islamic culture," and the Western powers' "extraordinary military might is seen as threatening and coercively dominating the Muslim world and propping up secular autocrats ready to accommodate the West."[15]

The Pew and PIPA findings underscore the difficulties Western policymakers face as they try to build new relationships with Muslim countries after the events of 2011. The changes that swept out old regimes did not sweep out mistrust of the West. Plenty of photographs remain in circulation showing Western leaders embracing Mubarak, flirting with Assad, and tolerating Qaddafi. The impact of those images will linger.

It should be kept in mind that this wariness is grounded in politics, as well as religion. Although Muslims are protective of their faith, most are also committed to political efforts that will help them to reach national and personal goals. In 2011, politics and Islam moved along different, if sometimes parallel, tracks in pursuit of regime change and reform.

Debate about these matters continues, with some theorists arguing that even those who cherish their religion are willing to balance that commitment with a certain amount of political pragmatism. Olivier Roy wrote that most of those involved in the uprisings of 2011 are part of a "post-Islamist generation." Others have very different views than those Roy has advanced, but he has argued that the generation that has been the driving force of the Arab Awakening has been "operating in a secular political space." One reason this could happen is that the reformers' movement toward democracy was home-grown, not imposed from outside as in the efforts by the George W. Bush administration to "democratize" Iraq. Because the roots of the movements that grew so rapidly in 2011 were in home soil, they had legitimacy.[16]

As the political characterization of "Islamists" has shifted toward moderation, wrote Roy, there is no longer a case to be made that "dictatorships are the most effective bulwark against Islamism; Islamists have become players in the democratic game." Economics is also a factor. Although compared with the sleek economies of many Western countries, the Arab states lag far behind. But in recent years, when growth rates in countries such as Egypt were around 5 percent, the middle class grew significantly larger and enjoyed the new economic stability. They have, not surprisingly, sought comparable political stability to protect their financial gains.[17]

Like any religion with a huge number of adherents (there are approximately 1.6 billion Muslims in the world), Islam continues to change, with numerous pressures—generational, economic, cultural—emanating from different parts of the globe and gradually reshaping the face and heart of the faith. These forces of change undermine the stereotypes that are so tempting partly because they allow quick judgments about people and events. But those who lapse into such judgments are almost certain to err in their responses to important political questions.

None of this is to minimize the importance of Islam in the Arab states or in the larger Muslim *ummah*. Rather, the point is that policymakers and others who evaluate events in predominantly Muslim countries should recognize that Islam, like so many other elements of modern life, is influenced by outside forces. Among the most important of these is the ability to consider a panoramic array of political options that various media forms have brought into view.

The Arab World Reborn

Perhaps Mohammed Bouazizi will be remembered as the Arab world's Rosa Parks. He decided that he had had enough. He refused to surrender his dignity, and the world changed.

The events that his suicide in Tunisia triggered showed, wrote Rami Khouri, that "the only serious mechanism for democratization is Arab public activism. It's not well-meaning foreign aid, not small groups of civil activists in our country trying this or trying that. And it's certainly not manipulating the public systems from the top. It's the public taking to the streets and demanding to change from autocratic to democratic systems."[18]

No one is quite certain about the route of the path to the tipping point. Bouazizi's suicide in itself was a sad act that might have attracted little notice had the reasons behind it not seemed so familiar to so many. Bouazizi was saying *"Kefaya"* (Enough) as had been said by so many others in the Arab states, and ignored by so many governments. But, finally, people took note. His voice, through his action, increased the volume of this cry to the point at which it could no longer be dismissed as inconsequential background noise. People listened and moved from a complaint, "Enough," to a demand, "The regime must go!"

As this cry was taken up throughout Arab countries, much of the rest of the world reacted first with surprise and then with a mixture of admiration, caution, and concern. US secretary of state Hillary Rodham Clinton saw an end to certain myths: "the myth that governments can hold on to power without responding to their people's aspirations or respecting their rights; the myth that the only way to produce change in the region is through violence and conflict; and, most pernicious of all, the myth that Arabs do not share universal human aspirations for freedom, dignity, and opportunity." As evidence of the demise of these myths, Clinton cited the Arab League's response to the uprising against Muammar Qaddafi, with the League affirming "the right of the Libyan people to fulfill their demands and build their own future and institutions in a democratic framework."[19] Such a pronouncement from what had long been a bastion of the Arab establishment would have been unthinkable just a few months earlier.

Rhetorical as well as material support from Clinton and Barack Obama was important, because the United States had a steep hill to climb to establish itself as a credible friend of the new Arab world. Arab publics are well aware of long-standing American backing for virtually every dictator in the region. Shadi Hamid observed, "America's unwillingness to align itself with democratic forces was not, it seemed, a matter of one president over another, but a structural problem inherent in U.S. foreign policy." Feelings about the United States develop on multiple levels. Hamid noted that "perceived U.S. bias toward Israel was central, but so too was the general sense that the West had blocked, sometimes purposefully, the natural development of an entire people and region. That reality put Arab opposition groups in the awkward situation of seeing America as the hope for democracy but, at the same time, hating it for falling so short."[20]

Meanwhile, Israel watched warily, particularly as the Mubarak regime fell in Egypt. Israel had no great love for Mubarak, but as was the case with most of the other Arab rulers, he was the devil they knew, and they had developed policy based on this knowledge. One unnamed Israeli official told the *New York Times* that "We are witnessing a paradigm shift in front of our eyes. Egypt was a major stabilizer in the region, and that may be over." Further, popular sentiment, which presumably would reflect little patience with Israel, was expected to play a greater role in Egyptian policy than it had during the Mubarak years.[21] To this, Rami Khouri added, "Definitely there will be more support for the Palestinian people, which will create more stress on Israel. There will probably be more clarity and diplomatic vigor in the Arab countries" in their dealings with Israel.[22]

Israel's supposed centrality in the Arab political consciousness was not much in evidence during the uprisings, and anti-Americanism also remained mostly beneath the surface. In a region that has for so long been seen as being both coveted and subjugated by outsiders, the Arab Spring was remarkable for its almost exclusively inward perspective.

Nevertheless, new governments will mean new policies, although there is little reason to expect the shifts to significantly destabilize regional equilibrium. Besides country-specific changes in Arab foreign affairs, the concept of "Arabness" may become more significant, assuming Arabs define what it means within the new political context. Will it be inclusive or sectarian? David Ignatius wrote that "The Arab transition needs to embrace the tolerance of secular societies rather than the intolerance of theocracy."[23] That approach, however, would take the transition into difficult terrain. To champion secularism would immediately be seen as a challenge to Islamic society and would produce pushback from conservatives. The task, difficult as it may be, is to create a society that emphasizes respectful tolerance without embracing a secularism that is seen as undermining religiosity. This can be done; Indonesia's political life during the past decade is worth studying for its relatively successful involvement of groups ranging from Islamists to strong secularists.[24]

Beyond religious issues, pan-Arabism is a sociopolitical goal that has long been discussed but has found little traction. It was advocated during the 1950s by Gamal Abdel Nasser, who used mass media tools such as his radio channel, Voice of the Arabs, to deliver political messages throughout the region. Al Jazeera is a descendant of Nasser's effort and has reinforced pan-Arabism by providing news from throughout the region and emphasizing that its coverage is not the product of a Western media giant but rather is news as seen by Arab eyes and related by Arab voices.

Al Jazeera's approach has been partly eclipsed by the current generation of young Arabs using the current generation of media tools. Hillary Clinton said that these young people "see alternatives, on satellite news, on Twitter and Facebook, in Cairo and Tunis. They know a better life can be within reach—and they are now willing to reach for it."[25] David Kirkpatrick and David Sanger wrote that a new force in the Arab world is a "pan-Arab youth movement dedicated to spreading democracy in a region without it." They added that these young people "fused their secular expertise in social networks with a discipline culled from religious movements and combined the energy of soccer fans with the sophistication of surgeons."[26]

This is yet another example of the dispersal of influence. Although Al Jazeera along with Al Arabiya maintain their standing as principal regional news purveyors, the new media universe is populated by millions of other disseminators of information. No one of these has power comparable to that of the satellite channel giants, but nevertheless—through their Tweets, Facebook postings, and other offerings—they have their own audiences, large and small. Their influence is likewise large and small, but it is undeniably present, a factor in the simultaneous revolutions that are remaking the Arab world.

Real-Time Diplomacy

Dictatorships work best in darkness; they capitalize on ignorance as well as fear. But today, more and more people know things, all kinds of things—political, cultural, social. They vacuum up information from an ever-growing universe of sources. Some of what they acquire is accurate, some of it not. Conversation, which is an essential element of democracy, is more pervasive and ranges farther afield than ever before. All this is a function of the connectivity enabled by social media along with other information and communication technologies.

As 2011 began, an estimated 5 billion mobile phones were in use, and 2 billion people had access to the Internet, with both numbers growing steadily.[27] With those tools in their hands, people are able to connect to one another through social media and create new kinds of communities. Egyptian filmmaker Amr Salama stated that "the role of social media is to get everyone to know that we all share the same problems, we all share the same needs, we're all asking for the same rights."[28]

Salama used Twitter to gather more than 300 gigabytes of video taken by participants in the demonstrations in Tahrir Square and elsewhere. During the early days of the Arab Spring in Egypt, the demonstrators had broadcast their videos—which they had shot using mobile phones and simple cameras—on the Internet and had shared them with Arab news channels, using so many venues that the government was unable to stifle their dissemination. Salama decided to pull them together to create a documentary.[29]

The sense of community and participation generated by social media use may also affect the way information is received. Sociologist Zeynep Tufekci wrote, "Television functions as a distancing technology while social media works in the opposite direction: through transparency of the process of narrative construction, through immediacy of the intermediaries, through removal of censorship over images and stories (television never shows the truly horrific pictures of war), and through person-to-person interactivity, social media news curation creates a sense of visceral and intimate connectivity, in direct contrast to television, which is explicitly constructed to separate the viewer from the events."[30] The distance between those who report the news through social media and those who receive it is narrower than that between news organizations and their audiences. The providers and recipients using social media belong to the same species; they are not "the journalists" and "the public," between whom a considerable divide often exists.

Yet another aspect of media-related political change is seen in a contrarian theory about the politically energizing effects of media-based social networks. Navid Hassanpour argued that the mass media, including social media, can make a person passive and more content to be an observer rather than a participant in political action. "Full connectivity in a social network," wrote Hassanpour, "sometimes can hinder collective action," and, therefore, the Mubarak government's disruption of mobile phone and Internet service in January 2011 could well have been counterproductive. According to Hassanpour, the shutdown gave apolitical citizens a better sense of the breadth of the unrest and "forced more face-to-face communication," because people had to go out into the streets to find out what was happening.[31] These personal contacts can be more energizing than reading bulletins on a mobile phone screen.

Considerable uncertainty exists about these matters, and it will take time to gather evidence related to theories about what social media and networks really do and don't do. Meanwhile, numerous governments, with varying degrees of enthusiasm, are adding social media to their array of diplomatic tools. As of 2010, the US State Department operated 230 Facebook accounts, 80 Twitter feeds, 55 YouTube channels, 40 Flickr pages, and 25 blogs,[32] and the department's commitment to social media continues to increase.

Even with all this going on, the integration of social and other new media into the foreign policymaking process remains incomplete, both in terms of using incoming information and producing an outgoing flow. The twenty-first-century diplomacy endorsed by Hillary Rodham Clinton and others includes government-to-public and public-to-public linkages in which new media connections will be essential. Anne-Marie Slaughter wrote of this: "That much broader concept opens the door to a do-it-yourself foreign policy, in which individuals and groups can invent and execute an idea—for good or ill—that can affect their own and other countries in ways that once only governments could." Slaughter cited "our need for a framework that moves beyond states and addresses both governments and societies."[33]

Constructing this framework is an essential task. The world is moving so fast that policymakers are in danger of falling farther and farther off the pace, and are unable to respond to events in timely fashion. Today, "timely" means real-time.

★   ★   ★

Democracy retains its allure, attracting those who hope for better lives. Prospects for democracy are enhanced by the conversation and information gathering that media—particularly social and other new media—facilitate. In the countries of the 2011 Arab Awakening, aspirations and hopes rose to new heights, and during the coming years one of the most important tasks of the world's already existing democracies will be to help ensure that the newly reborn Arab world does not slide off those heights.

The diplomacy involved in this will be challenging. It must embrace the new media that have been built into this century's emerging political processes while at the same time performing the traditional tasks of advancing national interests.

Moral sustenance for this work can be drawn from the ample supplies of courage on display in the aftermath of Mohamed Bouazizi's act of defiance. From the streets of Sidi Bouzid to Cairo's Tahrir Square and on to Manama, Sanaa, Damascus, Tripoli, and elsewhere—people were willing to risk the present in pursuit of the kind of future they wanted.

Many of these people became accustomed to the rapid pace at which events moved. Their uprisings were transformative in part because they were real-time revolutions, and the autocrats of the region were unable to adjust to this new political reality. As of this writing, some of these dictators have fallen and more may follow.

However the events in the individual Arab states turn out, it is certain that global politics and the related roles of media have been profoundly altered. The movement toward democracy in 2011 had centuries of tradition behind it, and in time it will be looked back upon as another important moment in humankind's unending pursuit of freedom. As these changes take hold, policymakers and publics throughout the world will undoubtedly adapt to the realities of real-time diplomacy.

AFTERWORD

The body of this book was written during the spring and summer of 2011, and this afterword is being composed in December of this remarkable year. It is always risky to try to write a contemporaneous account of a major change in the world and then wait for many months before it is published. Things that once seemed certain may have unraveled, and the course of events may have altered dramatically.

The Arab Awakening has encountered some difficult times since its early days, but democratic reform continues to move forward along its bumpy road. The most encouraging signs come from Tunisia, where open elections have kept the country on its path toward constitutional government. Egypt's path has been rockier, with the military unwilling to surrender its control even in the face of continuing protests. Muslim-Christian tensions have increased and candidates representing the Muslim Brotherhood and Salafi Islamists fared well in the first rounds of parliamentary elections. The Brotherhood, in particular, was able to reap the benefits of many years of political organizing. As is the case elsewhere in the region, the role of religion in Egypt's governance is being redefined.

An optimistic—but, hopefully, not wholly unrealistic—view of Egypt leads me to anticipate that the military will eventually give way to reform pressures and that the term "Islamist" will cease to be seen as a pejorative label. This latter point will require a readjustment of perspective on the part of the non-Muslim world—a better understanding of Islam and its role in political systems.

In Libya, Muammar Qaddafi is dead and the country is trying to create a new society without having any political infrastructure on which to build. At last report, approximately 125,000 men were under arms, split into a large array of militias. The volatility that inevitably accompanies such a situation poses a danger to the new state. But at least Libya, with its oil production, has an economic base that may provide some stability during its reconstruction.

In Yemen and Syria, bloodshed remains abundant as revolutions continue, with no happy endings in sight. Bahrain, Algeria, Jordan, Morocco, and perhaps other states are likely to see further turmoil. Saudi Arabia is still trying to decide how much reform it really wants to undertake. This regional giant will be watched closely by political observers as well as gerontologists.

All this hardly sounds hopeful, but it is worth heeding the words of Wael Ghonim, an important player in Egypt's uprising: "I believe that anyone participating in effecting change cannot be a pessimist. That is why, when it comes to Egypt's future, I am an optimist. Revolution is a process; its failure and success cannot be measured after only a few months, or even years. We must continue to believe."[1]

As revolutionary politics continue to evolve, so too does the technology that assisted the Arab Awakening. The increasing ubiquity of mobile phones is a good example of this. Throughout the world, more than 100,000 new mobile phone masts are erected each year (including one installed by the Chinese at the Mount Everest base camp, so if you're climbing Everest you can call home). The continent with the fastest growth of this technology is Africa, where mobile phone penetration has risen from 2 percent in 2010 to more than 30 percent today. Investment of US$50 billion in cellular infrastructure in sub-Saharan Africa will change the nature of communication in most countries there.[2]

Illustrating the connection between communication technology and politics, speculation has begun about a "sub-Saharan Spring," that presumably would take advantage of this spreading mobile phone usage. First stirrings have occurred in Burkina Faso and Uganda, and in countries such as Angola, Equatorial Guinea, and Zimbabwe, antigovernment groups have taken note of what their Arab neighbors have done.[3]

The political and intellectual empowerment that social media stimulate will make its presence felt as mobile technology, broadband Internet, and other new media technologies spread throughout the world. People will use Twitter, Facebook, and still-to-be-invented tools that will allow them to communicate within new community networks. Activists will be more aware of the politics of their own countries and those of other nations. What will they do about it? In December 2011, the Egyptian Facebook page "We Are All Khaled Said" offered this message: "Twenty thousand innocent Egyptians were in Mubarak jails being tortured and held without trial for their political views, while the world was friends with Mubarak for 30 years because they thought a dictator can bring them stability. Do you think the world leaders will learn and stop supporting dictators regardless of their interests?"

An important question, without a ready answer. For all the friendly rhetoric about the Arab Awakening that emerged from the West and elsewhere, Egyptian reformers and others are wise to retain their suspicions of outsiders' motivations and the level of their potential support.

Diplomats throughout the world, most of whom were caught unawares by the events of 2011, are still trying to figure out how to reconcile the tasks of diplomacy with the technological exigencies that now so profoundly affect their jobs. They all would acknowledge that information is power, but many would only grudgingly accept the idea that information is democratizing the ways that foreign policy is designed and conducted. Popular participation in the back-and-forth flow of information will increase, as will the speed of the process. Crafting successful foreign policy in the years ahead will depend on governments' willingness to accept the transformative combination of new politics, new technologies, and new participation. all of these are elements of real-time diplomacy.

For those who will write histories of this exciting time, the Arab Awakening will stand less as a triumph of technology than as an example of how people of courage can assert control over their own lives. A shining personification of this is Tawakkol Karman, the young Yemeni activist who was cowinner of the 2011 Nobel Peace Prize. In her Nobel lecture, Karman said: "The Arab people have woken up just to see how poor a share of freedom, democracy, and dignity they have." As a result, she said, "young Arab people, women and men, march in peaceful demonstrations demanding freedom and dignity from their rulers. . . . They march in a dramatic scene which embodies the most beautiful of the human spirit of sacrifice and the aspiration to freedom and life, against the ugliest forms of selfishness, injustice, and the desire to hold on to power and wealth."[4]

There you have it—the commitment and idealism that will change the world and will challenge those who must manage real-time diplomacy.

NOTES

Introduction

1. Jeffrey Ghannam, "Social Media in the Arab World: Leading Up to the Uprisings of 2011," Center for International Media Assistance, National Endowment for Democracy, February 3, 2011, 30.
2. Robert Darnton, *Poetry and the Police: Communication Networks in Eighteenth-Century Paris* (Cambridge, MA: Harvard University Press, 2010), 1.
3. Robert Darnton, "Five Myths of the 'Information Age'," *Chronicle of Higher Education,* April 22, 2011, B 9.
4. Jeffrey Ghannam, "In the Middle East, This Is Not a Facebook Revolution," *Washington Post,* February 18, 2011.
5. Frank Rich, "Wallflowers at the Revolution," *New York Times,* February 5, 2011.
6. David Ottaway and Marina Ottaway, "Of Revolutions, Regime Change, and State Collapse in the Arab World," http://www.wilsoncenter.org/index.cfmtopic_id=1426&fuseaction=topics.item&news_id=654739.
7. http://www.bbc.co.uk/news/10569081.
8. Malcolm Gladwell, "Small Change: Why the Revolution Will Not Be Tweeted," *New Yorker,* October 4, 2010.
9. Clay Shirky, "From Innovation to Revolution: Do Social Media Make Protests Possible?" *Foreign Affairs,* Vol. 90, No. 2, March/April 2011, 154.
10. Manuel Castells, *Communication Power* (Oxford: Oxford University Press, 2009), 21.
11. Ibid., 23.

1   The Political Revolution

1. http://www.whitehouse.gov/the-press-office/2011/02/11/remarks-president-egypt (accessed July 24, 2011).

2. Robin Wright, *Rock the Casbah: Rage and Rebellion across the Islamic World* (New York: Simon & Schuster, 2011), 16.

3. http://www.internetworldstats.com/africa.htm (accessed July 24, 2011).

4. *The New Arab Revolt* (New York: Council on Foreign Relations and *Foreign Affairs,* 2011), 404–407.

5. Steve Coll, "The Casbah Coalition: Tunisia's Second Revolution," *New Yorker,* April 4, 2011, 40.

6. Michele Penner Angrist, "Morning in Tunisia: The Frustrations of the Arab World Boil Over," in *The New Arab Revolt,* 76–77.

7. Marc Lynch, "The Wages of Arab Decay," in Marc Lynch, Susan B. Glasser, and Blake Hounshell (eds.), *Revolution in the Arab World* (Washington: Slate Group, 2011), 42.

8. Peter Coy, "A Message from the Street," *Bloomberg Businessweek,* February 7, 2011, 63.

9. Rami G. Khouri, "The Long Revolt," *Wilson Quarterly,* vol. 35, no. 3, Summer 2011, 44.

10. Lisa Anderson, "Demystifying the Arab Spring," *Foreign Affairs,* vol. 90, no. 3, May/June 2011, 3; Tom Malinowski, "Did WikiLeaks Take Down Tunisia's Government," in Lynch, Glasser, and Hounshell, *Revolution in the Arab World,* 57.

11. Wright, *Rock the Casbah,* 2, 42, 46.

12. David B. Ottaway, "Morocco's Arab Spring," Woodrow Wilson International Center for Scholars, June 22, 2011, http://www.wilson center.org/article/moroccos-arab-spring (accessed July 15, 2011).

13. Richard Auxler, "Egypt, Democracy and Islam," Pew Research Center, January 31, 2011, http://pewresearch.org/pubs/1874 /egypt-protests-democracy-islam-influence-politics-islam (accessed January 31, 2011).

14. "Excerpts from the Sermon of Shaykh Yusuf al-Qaradawi," in *New Arab Revolt,* 426.

15. "Holy Smoke," *Economist,* October 29, 2011, 72.

16. Samantha M. Shapiro, "Ministering to the Upwardly Mobile Muslim," *New York Times Magazine,* April 30, 2006.

17. Ethar El-Katatney, "Faith and Hope in Egypt: Interview with Amr Khaled," *Cairo Review of Global Affairs,* no. 1, Spring 2011, 69.

18. Ibid., 71.

19. John L. Esposito, *The Future of Islam* (New York: Oxford University Press, 2010), 134.

20. "Popular Protest in North Africa and the Middle East (I): Egypt Victorious?" International Crisis Group, Middle East/North Africa Report no. 101, February 24, 2011, 23–24.

21. Charles Hirschkind, "The Road to Tahrir," "The Immanent Frame," Social Science Research Council, February 9, 2011, http://blogs.ssrc .org/tif/2011/02/09/the-road-to-tahrir (accessed February 9, 2011).

22. Shadi Hamid, "The Rise of the Islamists," *Foreign Affairs,* vol. 90, no. 3, May/June 2011, 47.

23. "Uneasy Companions," *Economist,* August 6, 2011, 21.

24. Aaron David Miller, "For America, an Arab Winter," *Wilson Quarterly,* vol. 35, no. 3, Summer 2011, 40.

25. Nadia Al-Sakkaf, "Yemen's Outstanding Women," *Yemen Times,* July 25, 2011, http://www.yementimes.com/defaultdet.aspx?SUB _ID=36376 (accessed July 31, 2011).

26. Wright, *Rock the Casbah,* 155.

27. Leila Ahmed, "Veil of Ignorance?" *Foreign Policy,* May/June 2011, 41.

28. Wendell Steavenson, "Who Owns the Revolution?" *New Yorker,* August 1, 2011, 40.

29. Miller, "For America, an Arab Winter," 36.

30. Charles Levinson and Margaret Coker, "The Secret Rally that Sparked an Uprising," *Wall Street Journal,* February 11, 2011.

31. "Popular Protest in North Africa and the Middle East," 4.

32. Ibid. 19–20.

33. Jack A. Goldstone, "Understanding the Revolutions of 2011," *Foreign Affairs,* vol. 90, no. 3, 8, May/June 2011.

34. "Popular Protest in North Africa and the Middle East," 15.

35. Helene Cooper, "With Egypt, Diplomatic Words Often Fail," *New York Times,* January 29, 2011.

36. http://www.state.gov/secretary/rm/2011/01/155280.htm (accessed August 1, 2011).

37. Ryan Lizza, "The Consequentialist: How the Arab Spring Remade Obama's Foreign Policy," *New Yorker,* May 2, 2011, 51.

38. Ibid., 52.

39. Ibid., 53.

40. Aaron David Miller, "Cairo Wasn't Obama's to Lose," in Lynch, Glasser, and Hounshell, *Revolution in the Arab World,* 195.

41. "Throwing Money at the Street," *Economist,* March 12, 2011, 32.

42. Adam Baron, "Latest Word from Yemen's Ill President Doesn't Allay Tensions," *Miami Herald,* August 3, 2011.

43. http://www.whitehouse.gov/the-press-office/2011/07/31 /statement-president-violence-syria.

44. *The White House Blog,* August 18, 2011, http://www.whitehouse .gov/blog/2011/08/18/president-obama-future-syria-must -be-determined-its-people-president-bashar-al-assad (accessed September 1, 2011).

45. Thomas L. Friedman, "The New Hama Rules," *New York Times,* August 3, 2011.

2   The Media Revolution

1. Rami G. Khouri, "When Arabs Tweet," *New York Times,* July 22, 2010.
2. Josh Halliday, "Hillary Clinton Adviser Compares Internet to Che Guevara," *guardian.co.uk,* June 22, 2010, http://www.guardian.co.uk/media/2011/jun/22/hillary-clinton-adviser-alec-ross/ (accessed June 23, 2011).
3. Quoted in Shanthi Kalathil and Taylor C. Boas, *Open Networks, Closed Regimes* (Washington: Carnegie Endowment for International Peace, 2003), 1.
4. Mohammed El Oifi, "Influence without Power: Al Jazeera and the Arab Public Sphere," in Zayani, *The Al Jazeera Phenomenon,* 72.
5. Lawrence Pintak, "Reporting the Revolution: The New Voice of Arab Journalism," *Layalina Perspectives,* vol. 3, issue 1, January 2011, 1.
6. Lawrence Pintak, "Breathing Room: Toward a New Arab Media," *Columbia Journalism Review,* May/June 2011, 24.
7. Ibid., 25.
8. Jon Jensen, "Egypt's Youth Continue Their Fight on the Airwaves," *GlobalPost,* July 19, 2011, http://www.globalpost.com/dispatch/news/regions/middle-east/egypt/110718/egypt-youth-revolution-press (accessed July 20, 2011).
9. "Global Mobile Statistics 2011," http://mobithinking.com/mobile-marketing-tools/latest-mobile-stats#mobile-basics (accessed September 14, 2011).
10. Jennifer Preston and Brian Stelter, "Cellphones Become the World's Eyes and Ears on Protests," *New York Times,* February 18, 2011.
11. Philip Seib, *Beyond the Front Lines: How the News Media Cover a World Shaped by War* (New York: Palgrave Macmillan, 2004), 93–95.
12. Howard Kurtz,"Webloggers Signing On as War Correspondents," *Washington Post,* March 23, 2003.
13. Jennifer Preston, "When Unrest Stirs, Bloggers Are Already in Place," *New York Times,* March 13, 2011.
14. http://www.facebook.com/elshaheeed.co.uk
15. Romesh Ratnesar, "Not Just the Facebook Revolution," *Bloomberg Businessweek,* June 6, 2011, 64.
16. "Back to the Coffee House," *Economist,* July 9, 2011, 11.
17. Simon Cottle, "Media and the Arab Uprisings of 2011: Research Notes," *Journalism,* vol. 12, no. 5, 650.

18. Arab Advisors Group news releases: "Governments Continue to Dominate Terrestrial TV Channels in the Arab World," January 11, 2011, http://arabadvisors.com/pressers/presser-110111 (accessed February 24, 2011); "Egypt and Saudi Arabia, Followed by the UAE, Host the Highest Number of FTA Channels Broadcasting in the Arab World," June 21, 2011, http://www.arabadvisors.com /Pressers/presser-200611.htm (accessed June 22, 2011).

19. Julie Ray, "Young Arabs More Connected in 2010," Gallup, Inc. news release, April 11, 2011, http://www.gallup.com/poll/147035 /young-arabs-connected-2010 (accessed April 13, 2011).

20. Ibid.

21. Internet World Stats, "Internet Usage in the Middle East," http:// www.internetworldstats.com/stats5.htm (accessed August 7, 2011); "Internet Usage in Africa," http://www.internetworldstats.com /stats1.htm (accessed August 7, 2011).

22. Dubai School of Government, *Arab Social Media Report*, vol. 1, no. 2, May 2011, 9.

23. Ibid., 16.

24. Hayley Tsukayama, "Women's World Cup Sets Twitter Record," *washingtonpost.com,* http://www.washingtonpost.com /blogs/faster-forward/post/womens-world-cup-sets-twitter -record/2011/07/18/gIQAW4pdLI_blog.html (accessed August 7, 2011).

25. Maryam Ishani, "The Hopeful Network, *foreignpolicy.com,* February 7, 2011, http://www.foreignpolicy.com/artiles/2011/02/07/the_hope ful_network%23.tg-wyhtqcxl (accessed June 29, 2011).

26. Hirschkind, "The Road to Tahrir."

27. Sahar Khamis and Katherine Vaughn, "Cyberactivism in the Egyptian Revolution: How Civic Engagement and Citizen Journalism Tilted the Balance," *Arab Media and Society,* Summer 2011, no. 13, 8, http://www.arabmediasociety.com/article=769 (accessed May 31, 2011).

28. David D. Kirkpatrick and David E. Sanger, "A Tunisian-Egyptian Link that Shook Arab History," *New York Times,* February 13, 2011.

29. Khamis and Vaughn, "Cyberactivism in the Egyptian Revolution," 9.

30. Malek Mustafa, quoted in "Egypt Unreast: Bloggers Take Campaign to Tahrir Square," BBC News, February 7, 2011, http://www.bbc .co.uk/news/world-middle-east-12381295 (accessed February 7, 2011).

31. "Popular Protest in North Africa and the Middle East (1)," 8.

32. Matt Bradley and Summer Said, "State TV's Uncritical Coverage Draws Fire," *Wall Street Journal,* February 7, 2011.

33. L. Gordon Crovitz, "The Technology of Counterrevolution," *Wall Street Journal,* February 7, 2011.

34. James Glanz and John Markoff, "Egypt Leaders Found 'Off' Switch for Internet," *New York Times,* February 15, 2011.

35. "Popular Protest in North Africa and the Middle East (1)," 13, 19.

36. Nour Malas, "Syria Revolt Fueled by Roof Fires and Tweets," *Wall Street Journal,* July 15, 2011.

37. http://shaam.org/.

38. Malas, "Syria Revolt Fueled by Roof Fires and Tweets"; Hugh Macleod, "Syria's Young Cyber Activists Keep Protests in View," *guardian.co,* April 15, 2011, http://www.guardian.co .uk/world/2011/apr/15/syria-activists-protests-in-view (accessed April 21, 2011); Liam Stack, "Activists Using Video To Bear Witness in Syria," *New York Times,* June 18, 2011.

39. http://www.facebook.com/president.al.asad?ref=ts.

40. "Social Media: A Double-Edged Sword in Syria," Reuters, July 13, 2011, http://www.reuters.com/article/2011/07/13/us-syria-social -media-idUSTRE76C3DB20110713 (accessed July 14, 2011).

41. Margaret Coker and Charles Levinson, "Rebels Hijack Gadhafi's Phone Network," *Wall Street Journal,* April 13, 2011.

42. Paul Sonne and Margaret Coker, "Firms Aided Libyan Spies," *Wall Street Journal,* August 30, 2011.

43. Magdalena Maria Karolak, "Civil Society and Web 2.0 Technology: Social Media in Bahrain," *Arab Media and Society,* no. 13, Summer 2011, http://www,arabmediasociety.com/index.php?article=773 (accessed May 31, 2011).

44. Cited in Philip Seib, *The Al Jazeera Effect* (Washington, DC: Potomac Books, 2008), 164.

45. Joshua Teitelbaum, "Saudi Arabia Contends with the Social Media Challenge," Jerusalem Center for Public Affairs, *Jerusalem Issue Briefs,* vol. 10, no. 28, February 8, 2011, http://www.jcpa.org /JCPA/Templates/ShowPage.asp?DBID=1&LNGID=1&TMID =111&FID=442&PID=0&IID=6006 (accessed February 8, 2011).

46. Neil MacFarquhar, "Social Media Help Keep the Door Open to Sustained Dissent Inside Saudi Arabia," *New York Times,* June 15, 2011.

47. David E. Miller, "Palestinians Bemoan Failure to Exploit Social Media," *Arab News,* May 19, 2011, http://arabnews.com/middle east/article415256.ece (accessed May 23, 2011).

48. Golnaz Esfandiari, "The Twitter Devolution," *Foreign Policy,* June 7, 2010, http://www.foreignpolicy.com/articles/2010/06/07 /the_twitter_revolution_that_wasnt (accessed July 8, 2011).

49. Ibid.

50. Joshua Keating, "Should U.S. Intelligence Be Paying More Attention to Twitter?" *foreignpolicy.com,* February 8, 2011, http://blog.foreignpolicy.com/posts/2011/02/08/should_us_intelligence_be_paying_more_attention_to_twitter (accessed June 29, 2011).

51. Richard Fontaine and Will Rogers, *Internet Freedom: A Foreign Policy Imperative in the Digital Age* (Washington, DC: Center for a New American Security, 2011), 25.

52. Ibid., 6.

53. Philip Seib and Dana Janbek, *Global Terrorism and New Media* (London: Routledge, 2011), ix.

54. Crovitz, "The Technology of Counterrevolution."

55. Josh Rogin, "Inside the State Department's Arab Twitter Diplomacy," *foreignpolicy.com,* January 28, 2011, http://thecable.foreignpolicy.com/posts/2011/01/28/inside_the_state_department_s_arab_twitter_diplomacy (accessed June 29, 2011).

56. http://millatfacebook.com/about.

57. "Pakistanis Create Rival Muslim Facebook," *dawn.com,* May 28, 2010, http://archives.dawn.com/archives/121487 (accessed August 11, 2011).

58. Haider Warraich, "Pakistan's Social Media Landscape," *foreign policy.com,* March 18, 2011, http://afpak.foreignpolicy.com/posts/2011/03/18/pakistans_social_media_landscape (accessed July 2, 2011).

59. http://www.internetworldstats.com/stats3.htm.

60. Jeremy Page, "China Co-opts Social Media to Head Off Unrest," *Wall Street Journal,* February 22, 2011.

61. James Fallows, "Arab Spring, Chinese Winter," *Atlantic,* September 2011, 50, 52.

62. Ibid., 53.

63. Crovitz, "The Technology of Counterrevolution."

3 Traditional Diplomacy and the Cushion of Time

1. Av Westin, *Newswatch* (New York: Simon & Schuster, 1982), 22.

2. "Commuting Ended: Warsaw Pact States Say Allies' Routes Remain Open," *New York Times,* August 13, 1961.

3. Harry Gilroy, "Mood of Berlin: Controlled Fury"; Seymour Topping, "Closing of Border Is Seen as First of Soviet Moves"; "U.S. Statement by Rusk," *New York Times,* August 14, 1961.

4. "Nothing to Lose But Chains" (editorial), *New York Times,* August 14, 1961.

5. "Berlin, the Testing Ground," *New York Times,* August 15, 1961.

6. Richard Reeves, *President Kennedy: Profile of Power* (New York: Simon & Schuster, 1993), 210.

7. Ibid., 212.

8. Max Frankel, "Reds Held Losing: Washington To Stress East German Move Confesses Failure," *New York Times,* August 16, 1961.

9. Theodore C. Sorensen, *Kennedy* (New York: Bantam, 1966), 669.

10. Dean Acheson, *Present at the Creation* (New York: Norton, 1969), 731.

11. George F. Kennan, *American Diplomacy* (New York: New American Library/Mentor, 1952), 91–92.

12. George F. Kennan, *At a Century's Ending: Reflections, 1982–1995* (New York: W. W. Norton, 1996), 297.

13. James A. Baker III, *The Politics of Diplomacy: Revolution, War & Peace, 1989–1992* (New York: Putnam, 1995), 361.

14. Ibid., 364.

15. David Hackett Fischer, *Paul Revere's Ride* (New York: Oxford University Press, 1994), 324–325.

16. John Ferling, *Independence: The Struggle to Set America Free* (New York: Bloomsbury Press, 2011), 121.

17. Ibid., 122.

18. Paul W. White, *News on the Air* (New York: Harcourt Brace, 1947), 31.

19. Alexander Kendrick, *Prime Time: The Life of Edward R. Murrow* (Boston: Little, Brown, 1969), 176.

20. Archibald MacLeish, "A Superstition Is Destroyed," in "In Honor of a Man and an Ideal: Three Talks on Freedom," CBS (privately printed), December 2, 1941, 7.

21. Hadley Cantril, "Public Opinion in Flux," *Annals of the American Academy of Political and Social Science,* vol. 220 (March 1942), 138. See also Philip Seib, *Broadcasts from the Blitz: How Edward R. Murrow Helped Lead America into War* (Washington: Potomac Books, 2006), 151–155.

22. Michael Arlen, *Living-Room War* (New York: Penguin, 1982), 82.

23. Ibid., 83.

24. Clark Clifford, *Counsel to the President* (New York: Random House, 1991), 474.

25. Daniel Hallin, *The "Uncensored War"* (Berkeley: University of California Press, 1989), 173. See also, Philip Seib, *Headline*

Diplomacy: How News Coverage Affects Foreign Policy (Westport, CT: Praeger, 1997), 16–28.

26. Quoted in Don Oberdorfer, *Tet* (New York: Avon, 1972), 264.

27. Quoted in Robert J. Donovan and Ray Scherer, *Unsilent Revolution* (New York: Cambridge University Press, 1992), 102.

28. Lyndon Baines Johnson, *The Vantage Point* (New York: Holt, Rinehart, and Winston, 1971), 384.

29. Quoted in Austin Ranney, *Channels of Power* (New York: Basic Books, 1983), 134.

30. Quoted in Robert Wiener, *Live from Baghdad* (New York: Doubleday, 1992), 253.

31. Quoted in Donovan and Sherer, *Unsilent Revolution,* 314.

32. Lawrence Grossman, "A Television Plan for the Next War," *Nieman Reports,* Summer 1991, 27.

33. Walter Goodman, "Many Big Stories to Tell, but the Biggest of All Is China," *New York Times,* June 5, 1989.

34. Lewis A. Friedland, *Covering the World* (New York: Twentieth Century Fund, 1992), 6.

35. Reuven Frank, "On Tiananmen Square, Echoes of Chicago in '68," *New York Times,* June 4, 1989.

4 The Arrival of Rapid-Reaction Diplomacy

1. Quoted in Robin Wright, *Rock the Casbah: Rage and Rebellion across the Islamic World* (New York: Simon & Schuster, 2011), 97–98.

2. Claudine Beaumont, "Mumbai Attacks: Twitter and Flickr Used to Break News," *Telegraph,* November 27, 2008.

3. Brian Stelter and Noam Cohen, "Citizen Journalists Provided Glimpses of Mumbai Attacks," *New York Times,* November 29, 2008.

4. Evgeny Morozov, "More Analysis of Twitter's Role in Moldova," ForeignPolicy.com, April 7, 2009, http://neteffect.foreignpolicy .com/posts/2009/04/07/more_analysis_of_twitters_role_in _moldova (accessed May 30, 2011).

5. Joel Schectman, "Iran's Twitter Revolution? Maybe Not Yet," *Bloomberg Businessweek,* June 17, 2009.

6. Anne Applebaum, "The Twitter Revolution that Wasn't," *Washington Post,* April 21, 2009.

7. Lev Grossman, "Iran Protests: Twitter, the Medium of the Movement," *Time,* June 17, 2009.

8. Patrick W. Quirk, "Iran's Twitter Revolution," *Foreign Policy in Focus,* June 17, 2009.

9. Mark Landler and Brian Stelter, "Washington Taps Into a Potent New Force in Diplomacy," *New York Times,* June 17, 2009.

10. Brad Stone and Noam Cohen, "Social Networks Spread Defiance Online," *New York Times,* June 16, 2009.

11. Schectman, "Iran's Twitter Revolution?"; Matthew Weaver, "Iran's 'Twitter Revolution' Was Exaggerated, Says Editor," *Guardian,* June 9, 2010.

12. Noam Cohen, "Twitter on the Barricades: Six Lessons Learned," *New York Times,* June 20, 2009.

13. Brian Stelter, "Journalism Rules Are Bent in News Coverage from Iran," *New York Times,* June 29, 2009.

14. James Poniewozik, "Iranians Protest Election, Tweeps Protest CNN," Time.com, June 15, 2009, http://tunedin.blogs.time.com /2009/06/15/iranians-protest-election-tweeps-protest-cnn/ (accessed May 29, 2011).

15. Jared Keller, "Evaluating Iran's Twitter Revolution," theatlantic .com, June 18, 2010, http://www.theatlantic.com/technology /archive/2010/06/evaluating-irans-twitter-revolution/58337/ (accessed May 29, 2011).

16. http://www.youtube.com/t/press.

17. Robin Wright, *Rock the Casbah,* 101–102.

18. Mette Mortensen, "When Citizen Journalism Sets the News Agenda: Neda Agha Soltan as a Web 2.0 Icon of Post-election Unrest in Iran," *Global Media and Communication,* vol. 7, no. 1, April 2011, 7–8.

19. http://www.internetworldstats.com/middle.htm#ir.

20. Christopher Rhoads and Farnaz Fassihi, "Iran Vows to Unplug Internet," *Wall Street Journal,* May 28, 2011.

21. Elias Biryaberema, "Uganda Bans SMS Texting of Key Words during Poll," Reuters Africa, February 17, 2011, http://af.reuters .com/article/ugandaNews/idAFLDE71G1Z620110217?sp=true (accessed June 9, 2011).

22. "Vodafone: Egypt Forced Us to Send Text Messages," ABC News, http://abcnews.go.com/technology/wirestory?id=12830205 (accessed June 9, 2011).

23. http://www.washingtonpost.com/world/autocratic-regimes -fight-web-savvy-opponents-with-their-own-tools/2011/04/19 /AFTfEN9G_print.html (accessed June 15, 2011).

24. http://en.wikipedia.org/wiki/Skype.

25. Steve Strecklow, Paul Sonne, and Matt Bradley, "Mideast Uses Western Tools to Battle the Skype Rebellion," *Wall Street Journal,* June 1, 2011.

26. Esther Adley, "Syrain Lesbian Blogger Is Revealed Conclusively to Be a Married Man," *Guardian,* June 13, 2011; David Kenner, "Straight Guy in Scotland," *ForeignPolicy.com,* http://www.foreign policy.com/articles/2011/06/13/straight_guy_in_scotland?print (accessed June 14, 2011).

27. James Glanz and John Markoff, "U.S. Underwrites Internet Detour around Censors," *New York Times,* June 12, 2011.

28. Glanz and Markoff, "U.S. Underwrites Internet Detour"; Kit Eaton, "Unpacking the Secret $2 Million Internet in a Suitcase," *Fastcompany.com,* June 13, 2011, http://www.fastcompany.com /1759428/unpacking-the-tech-of-the-secret-internet-in-a -suitcase.

29. http://www.whitehouse.gov/blog/2009/06/23/presidents -opening-remarks-iran-with-persian-translation (accessed June 1, 2011).

30. http://www.cbsnews.com/8301-503543_162-5106492-503543 .html (accessed June 3, 2011).

31. http://www.whitehouse.gov/the-press-office/2010/11/28 /statement-press-secretary (accessed June 3, 2011).

32. http://www.whitehouse.gov/the-press-office/2010/11/29/press -briefing-press-secretary-robert-gibbs-11292010 (accessed June 3, 2011).

33. http://www.state.gov/secretary/rm/2010/11/152078.htm (accessed June 3, 2011).

34. Christian Caryl, "WikiLeaks vs. U.S. Diplomacy," Radio Free Europe/Radio Liberty, December 1, 2010, http://www.rferl.org /content/wikileaks_assange_united_states_diplomacy/2236114 .html (accessed May 23, 2011).

5 The Expeditionary Diplomat and the Case for Public Diplomacy

1. Harold Nicolson, *Diplomacy* (Second Edition) (London: Oxford University Press, 1950), 168–169.

2. Blake Hounshell, "Henry Kissinger," *Foreign Policy,* July/August 2011, 28.

3. Marc Grossman, "Diplomacy Before and After Conflict," *Prism* (National Defense University), vol. 1, no. 4, September 2010, 12.

4. Brian Solis, "A Social Democracy: The White House Learns to Listen," *Fastcompany.com,* June 14, 2011, http://www.fastcompany .com/1759871/a-social-democracy-the-white-house-learns-to -listen (accessed June 16, 2011).

5. James Kitfield, "I Tweet for Freedom," *NationalJournal.com,* June 29, 2011, www.nationaljournal.com/i-tweet-for-freedom-20110629 (accessed July 15, 2011).

6. Walter Pincus, "State Dept. Tries Blog Diplomacy," *Washington Post,* November 19, 2007.

7. "Ambassador Robert Ford's Interview with Christiane Amanpour of ABC's *This Week,*" August 7, 2011, U.S. Department of State, www.state.gov/r/pa/prs/ps/2011/08/170033 (accessed September 1, 2011).

8. Ted Sorensen, *Counselor* (New York: HarperCollins, 2008), 331.

9. Charles Kenny, "Corps Concerns," *Foreign Policy,* www.foreign policy.com/articles/2011/02/22/corps_concerns (accessed June 29, 2011).

10. Ibid.

11. Philip Seib, "AIDS and Public Diplomacy," Center on Public Diplomacy, University of Southern California, http://uscpublic diplomacy.org/index.php/newswire/cpdblog_detail/aids_and _public_diplomacy.

12. Tommy G. Thompson, "Health Diplomacy Is Critical to U.S. Foreign Policy," *Huffington Post,* February 15, 2011, www .huffingtonpost.com/tommy-g-thompson/the-case-for-health -diplo_b_823382 (accessed June 27, 2011).

13. http://www.whitehouse.gov/the-press-office/remarks-president -cairo-university-6-04-09.

14. Adolf Hitler, *Mein Kamp* (translated into English by James Murphy), (London: Hurst and Blackett, 1939), Ch. 6, http://gutenberg.net .au/ebooks02/0200601.txt.

15. Edward R. Murrow, *This Is London* (New York: Simon & Schuster, 1941), 75.

16. Charles J. Rolo, *Radio Goes to War* (New York: G. P. Putnam's Sons, 1942), 70, 75.

17. Ibid., 76.

18. Harold N. Graves, Jr., "European Radio and the War," *Annals of the American Academy of Political and Social Science,* vol. 213 (January 1941), 80.

19. Harold N. Graves, Jr., "Propaganda by Short Wave: Berlin Calling America," *Public Opinion Quarterly,* vol. 4, no. 4, December 1940, 601, 602, 605, 606.

20. Rolo, *Radio Goes to War,* 112.

21. Graves, "Propaganda by Short Wave: Berlin Calling," 601, 606.

22. Ibid., 607, 610.

23. Rolo, *Radio Goes to War,* 120.

24. Graves, "Propaganda by Short Wave: Berlin Calling," 611, 612.

25. Rolo, *Radio Goes to War,* 121.

26. Murrow, *This Is London,* 74.

27. See Philip Seib, *Broadcasts from the Blitz: How Edward R. Murrow Helped Lead America into War* (Washington, DC: Potomac Books, 2006).

28. Chris Stephen, Robert Tuttle, and Caroline Alexander, "Qatar May Win Big If Libyan Rebels Prevail," *Bloomberg Businessweek,* July 18, 2011, 15; Blake Hounshell, "The Revolution Will Soon Be Televised," *foreignpolicy.com,* March 28, 2011, www.foreign policy.com/articles/2011/03/28/the_revolution_will_soon_be _televised (accessed March 31, 2011).

29. Simeon Kerr, "Gamble on Libya Pays Off for Qatar," *Financial Times,* August 28, 2011, http://www.ft.com/intl/cms/s/0/f937f630 -d16c-11e0-89c0-00144feab49a.html#axzz1Y8LQWUYy (accessed August 29, 2011).

30. Shawn Powers and Eytan Gilboa, "The Public Diplomacy of Al Jazeera," in Philip Seib (ed.), *New Media and the New Middle East* (New York: Palgrave Macmillan, 2007), 74–75.

31. Will Wachter, "The Language of Chinese Soft Power in the U.S.," *Asia Times Online,* May 24, 2007, http://www.atimes.com/atimes /China/IE24Ad01.html (accessed June 25, 2011).

32. Jian Wang, "Public Diplomacy with Chinese Characteristics," *CPD Blog,* Center on Public Diplomacy, University of Southern California, May 4, 2011, http://uscpublicdiplomacy.org/index.php /newswire/cpdblog_detail/public_diplomacy_with_chinese _characteristics/ (accessed June 25, 2011).

33. Andrew Walker, "China's New Economic Power Fans Fear, BBC Poll Finds," BBC World Service, March 27, 2011, http://www .bbc.co.uk/news/business-12867892 (accessed June 25, 2011).

34. Mark Landler, "A New Voice of America for the Age of Twitter," *New York Times,* June 7, 2011.

35. David Saranga, "The Use of New Media in Public Diplomacy," *One Jerusalem,* June 3, 2009, http://www.onejerusalem.org/2009/06 /the-use-of-new-media-in-public.php (accessed July 8, 2011).

36. Lina Khatib, William Dutton, and Michael Thelwall, "Public Diplomacy 2.0: An Exploratory Case Study of the U.S. Digital Outreach Team," *CDDRL Working Papers,* no, 120, January 2011, Center on Democracy, Development, and the Rule of Law, Stanford University, 3, 6, 17, 23, 24, 26.

6 The Promise of Networks

1. Miriam Cooke and Bruce B. Lawrence, "Introduction," in Miriam Cooke and Bruce B. Lawrence (eds.), *Muslim Networks from Hajj to*

Hip Hop (Chapel Hill, NC: University of North Carolina Press, 2005), 1.

2. Amelia Arsenault, "Networks: The Technological and the Social," in Gerard Delanty and Steven Turner (eds.), *Handbook of Contemporary Social and Political Theory* (London: Routledge, 2011), 260.

3. Manuel Castells, *The Power of Identity* (Second Edition) (New York: Wiley-Blackwell, 2009), 304.

4. Clay Shirky, "The Political Power of Social Media," *Foreign Affairs,* vol. 90, no. 1, January/February 2011, 29.

5. Charlie Beckett, "After Tunisia and Egypt: Towards a New Typology of Media and Networked Political Change," *Polis,* London School of Economics and Political Science, February 11, 2011, http://blogs.lse.ac.uk/polis/2011/02/11/after-tunisia-and-egypt -towards-a-new-typology-of-media-and-networked-political -change/ (accessed August 14, 2011).

6. Castells, *Communication Power,* 120.

7. Manuel Castells, "Communication, Power, and Counter-Power in the Network Society," *International Journal of Communication,* 1, 2007, 246, 248.

8. Anne-Marie Slaughter, *A New World Order* (Princeton: Princeton University Press, 2004), 31.

9. Ibid., 4.

10. Ibid., 54.

11. Kenneth Weisbrode, "Diplomacy 2.0," *guardian.co,* March 28, 2010, http://www.guardian.co.uk/commentisfree/2010/mar/28 /diplomacy-technology.

12. Larry Diamond, "Liberation Technology," *Journal of Democracy,* vol. 21, no. 3, July 2010, 70.

13. Howard Rheingold, *Smart Mobs: The Next Social Revolution* (New York: Basic Books, 2003), 158.

14. Diamond, "Liberation Technology," 78; Manuel Castells, Mirela Fernandez-Ardevol, Jack Linchuan Qiu, and Araba Sey, "Electronic Communication and Socio-Political Mobilisation: A New Form of civil Society," in Marlies Glasius, Mary Kaldor, and Helmut Anheier (eds.), *Global Civil Society* (London: Sage, 2006), 112.

15. Castells, Fernandez-Ardevol, Qiu, and Sey, "Electronic Communication and Socio-Political Mobilisation," 112–114.

16. Ibid., 116.

17. Some of the following material is based on content in Seib, *The Al Jazeera Effect* and Seib and Janbek, *Global Terrorism and New Media.*

18. Abdel Bari Atwan, *The Secret History of al Qaeda* (Berkeley: University of California Press, 2006), 222.

19. National Commission on Terrorist Attacks upon the United States, *The 9/11 Commission Report* (New York: W. W. Norton, 2004), 362–363.

20. Faisal Devji, *Landscapes of the Jihad* (Ithaca, NY: Cornell University Press, 2005), 137.

21. Jason Burke, *Al Qaeda* (London: I. B. Tauris, 2003), 12.

22. National Commission on Terrorist Attacks, 145.

23. Michele Zanini and Sean J. A. Edwards, "The Networking of Terror in the Information Age," in John Arquila and David Ronfeldt (eds.), *Networks and Netwars* (Santa Monica: RAND, 2001), 34.

24. Gabriel Weimann, *Terror on the Internet* (Washington: United States Institute of Peace, 2006), 115–116.

25. Lawrence Wright, "The Terror Web," *New Yorker,* August 2, 2004, 44.

26. Weimann, *Terror on the Internet,* 66.

27. "Winning or Losing: A Special Report on Al Qaeda," *Economist,* July 19, 2008, 4–5.

28. Daniel Benjamin (panelist), "The United States vs. Al Qaeda," in Karen J. Greenberg (ed.), *Al Qaeda Now* (New York: Cambridge University Press, 2005), 106.

29. Patrick Radden Keefe, "Can Network Theory Thwart Terrorists?" *New York Times,* March 12, 2006.

30. Scott Shane, "As Regimes Fall in the Arab World, Al Qaeda Sees History Fly By," *New York Times,* February 27, 2011.

31. Ramy Raoof, "Mobile Tactics for Participants in Peaceful Assemblies," *mobileactive.org,* May 17, 2011, http://mobileactive. org/howtos/mobile-tactics-peaceful-assemblies (accessed June 9, 2011).

7   Ripple Effects

1. Volodymyr V. Lysenko and Kevin C. Desouza, "The Internet in the Orange Revolution in September–December 2004," *First Monday,* vol. 15, nos. 9–6, September 2010, http://firstmonday.org/htbin /cgiwrap/bin/ojs/index.php/fm/article/view/2992/2599 (accessed August 25, 2011.

2. Greg Satell, "Small Acts of Courage and Revolution," *digitaltonto,* October 24, 2010, http://www.digitaltonto.com/2010/small-acts -of-courage-and-revolution/ (accessed August 25, 2011).

3. Joshua Goldstein, "The Role of Digital Networked Technologies in the Ukrainian Orange Revolution," The Berkman Center for Internet & Society at Harvard Law School, Research Publication No. 2007-14, December 2007, 19.

4. Lysenko and Desouza, "The Internet in the Orange Revolution."
5. Goldstein, "The Role of Digital Networked Technologies," 4.
6. Ibid., 10.
7. Aaron Smith and Lee Rainie, *The Internet and the 2008 Election* (Washington: Pew Internet & American Life Project, 2008), i–iii.
8. Matthew Fraser and Soumitra Dutta, "Barack Obama and the Facebook Election," *usnews.com,* November 19, 2008, http://www.usnews.com/opinion/articles/2008/11/19/barack-obama-and-the-facebook-election (accessed August 22, 2011).
9. Jennifer Preston, "Republicans Sharpening Online Tools for 2012," *New York Times,* April 19, 2011.
10. "The Blackberry Riots," *Economist,* August 13, 2011, 52.
11. Evgeny Morozov, "Repressing the Internet, Western-Style," *Wall Street Journal,* August 13, 2011.
12. J. David Goodman, "In British Riots, Social Media and Face Masks Are the Focus," *nytimes.com,* August 11, 2011, http://thelede.blogs.nytimes.com/2011/08/11/social-media-and-facemasks-are-targets-after-british-riots/ (accessed August 22, 2011).
13. Ibid.
14. Robert Mackey, "Egyptian Bloggers Parse London Riots in Real Time," *nytimes.com,* August 8, 2011, http://thelede.blogs.nytimes.com/2011/08/08/egyptian-bloggers-parse-london-riots-in-real-time/ (accessed August 22, 2011).
15. "The Blackberry Riots," 52.
16. Morozov, "Repressing the Internet."
17. Ramesh Srinavasan, "London, Egypt, and the Nature of Social Media," *Washington Post,* August 11, 2011.
18. Morozov, "Repressing the Internet."
19. Evan Hill, "US Railway Blocked Phones to Quash Protest," *aljazeera.net,* August 13, 2011, http://english.aljazeera.net/news/americas/2011/08/201181221139693608.html (accessed August 16, 2011).
20. Jennifer Preston, "Riots Spread on Social Media, As Does the Cleanup," *newyorktimes.com,* August 9, 2011, http://mediadecoder.blogs.nytimes.com/2011/08/09/riots-spread-on-social-media-as-does-the-cleanup (accessed August 10, 2011).
21. http://wikileaks.org.
22. "A Note to Readers: The Decision To Publish Diplomatic Documents," *New York Times,* November 28, 2010.
23. "Swept Up and Away," *Economist,* September 10, 2011, 65.
24. "The Palestine Papers Fallout," Al Jazeera English, February 19, 2011, http://english.aljazeera.net/programmes/listeningpost/2011/02/2011219134917532278.html (accessed August 26, 2011).

25. Lee Bollinger, "News for the World," *Columbia Journalism Review,* July/August 2011, http://www.cjr.org/cover_story/news_for_the _world.php?page=all (accessed July 20, 2011).

8   Looking Ahead

1. Hillary Rodham Clinton, "Internet Rights and Wrongs: Choices and Challenges in a Networked World," speech at the George Washington University, February 15, 2011, http://www.state .gov/secretary/rm/2011/02/156619.htm# (accessed August 28, 2011).
2. Ibid.
3. Hal Roberts, Ethan Zuckerman, Robert Faris, Jillian York, and John Palfrey, "The Evolving Landscape of Internet Control," Berkman Center for Internet & Society, August 2011, 2, http://cyber.law .harvard.edu/sites/cyber.law.harvard.edu/files/Evolving_Land scape_of_Internet_Control_3.pdf (accessed August 25, 2011).
4. Roberts, Zuckerman, Faris, York, and Palfrey, "The Evolving Landscape," 8.
5. Hal Roberts, Ethan Zuckerman, Jillian York, Robert Faris, and John Palfrey, "International Bloggers and Internet Control," Berkman Center for Internet & Society, August 2011, 11, http://cyber.law .harvard.edu/sites/cyber.law.harvard.edu/files/International _Bloggers_and_Internet_Control_Results_0.pdf (accessed August 25, 2011).
6. Jim Cowie, "What Libya Learned from Egypt," *Huffington Post,* March 5, 2011, http://www.huffingtonpost.com/jim-cowie/libya -egypt-internet_b_831794.html (accessed September 9, 2011); Noam Cohen, "In Unsettled Times, Media Can Be a Call to Action, or a Distraction," *New York Times,* August 28, 2011.
7. Roberts, Zuckerman, York, Faris, and Palfrey, "International Bloggers and Internet Control," 11.
8. "Egyptian Military Court Sentences Blogger to Three Years," Associated Press, April 11, 2011, http://www.npr.org/2011/04/12 /135332506/egyptian-military-court-sentences-blogger (accessed April 14, 2011).
9. Eliza Griswold, *The Tenth Parallel* (New York: Farrar, Straus and Giroux, 2010), 130.
10. *Muslim-Western Tensions Persist* (Washington: Pew Research Center, 2011), 1.
11. Ibid.,16.
12. Ibid., 5.
13. Steven Kull, "Why Muslims Are Still Mad at America," cnn.com, September 5, 2011, http://globalpublicsquare.blogs.cnn.com/2011/09

/05/why-muslims-are-still-mad-at-america (accessed September 6, 2011).

14. *Muslim-Western Tensions Persist,* 16.

15. Kull, "Why Muslims Are Still Mad at America."

16. Olivier Roy, "This Is Not an Islamic Revolution," *New Statesman,* February 15, 2011, http://www.newstatesman.com /religion/2011/02/egypt-arab-tunisia-islamic (accessed August 29, 2011).

17. Ibid.

18. Scott MacLeod, "Region in Revolt: Interview with Rami G. Khouri," *Cairo Review of Global Affairs,* no. 1, Spring 2011, 126–127.

19. Hillary Rodham Clinton, "Remarks at the Gala Dinner Celebrating the U.S.-Islamic World Forum," April 12, 2011, http://www.state .gov/secretary/rm/2011/04/160642.htm (accessed September 6, 2011).

20. Shadi Hamid, "The Struggle for Middle East Democracy," *Cairo Review of Global Affairs,* no. 1, Spring 2011, 22, 24.

21. Ethan Bronner, "Israel Faces Painful Challenges as Ties Shift with Arab Neighbors in Upheaval," *New York Times,* August 27, 2011.

22. MacLeod, "Region in Revolt," 134.

23. David Ignatius, "An Uncertain Arab Transition," *Washington Post,* August 18, 2011.

24. Donald L. Horowitz, "Writing the New Rules of the Game," *Wilson Quarterly,* vol. 35, no. 3, Summer 2011, 54.

25. Clinton, "Remarks at the Gala Dinner Celebrating the U.S.-Islamic World Forum."

26. David D. Kirkpatrick and David E. Sanger, "A Tunisian-Egyptian Link that Shook Arab History," *New York Times,* February 13, 2011.

27. Eric Schmidt and Jared Cohen, "The Digital Disruption: Connectivity and the Diffusion of Power," *Foreign Affairs,* vol. 89, no. 6, November/December 2010, 75.

28. Tim Carmody, "Crowdsourcing the Documentary: Egyptian Filmmaker Uses Twitter to Gather 300 GB of Activist Video," *Fastcompany.com,* June 13, 2011, http://www.fastcompany.com /1759589/crowdsourcing-the-documentary-egyptian-filmmaker -uses-twitter-to-gather-300-gb-of-activist-video (accessed June 14, 2011).

29. Carmody, "Crowdsourcing the Documentary."

30. Zeynep Tufekci, "Twitter and the Anti-Playstation Effect on War Coverage," http://technosociology.org/?p=393 (accessed September 9, 2011).

31. Noam Cohen, "In Unsettled Times."

32. United States Government Accountability Office, *Engaging Foreign Audiences,* GAO 10-767, July 2010, 13–14.

33. Anne-Marie Slaughter, "The New Foreign Policy Frontier," *the-atlantic.com,* July 2011, http://www.theatlantic.com/international /archive/2011/07/the-new-foreign-policy-frontier/242593/ (accessed July 28, 2011).

Afterword

1. Wael Ghonim, "In Bleak Cairo, a Call for Optimism," *New York Times,* November 28, 2011.

2. Dale Peskin, "News on the Go: How Mobile Devices Are Changing the World's information Ecosystem" (Washington: Center for International Media Assistance/National Endowment for Democracy, 2011), 4.

3. "A Sub-Saharan Spring?" *Economist,* "The World in 2012," 76.

4. Tawakkol Karman, "Nobel Lecture," December 10, 2011, http://www.nobelprize.org/nobel_prizes/peace/laureates/2011 /karman-lecture_en.html.

INDEX